Social Network Analysis
for Startups

Maksim Tsvetovat and Alexander Kouznetsov

O'REILLY®

Beijing · Cambridge · Farnham · Köln · Sebastopol · Tokyo

Social Network Analysis for Startups

by Maksim Tsvetovat and Alexander Kouznetsov

Published by O'Reilly Media, Inc., 1005 Gravenstein Highway North, Sebastopol, CA 95472.

O'Reilly books may be purchased for educational, business, or sales promotional use. Online editions are also available for most titles (*http://my.safaribooksonline.com*). For more information, contact our corporate/institutional sales department: (800) 998-9938 or *corporate@oreilly.com*.

Editors:	Shawn Wallace and Mike Hendrickson	**Cover Designer:**	Karen Montgomery
Production Editor:	Kristen Borg	**Interior Designer:**	David Futato
Proofreader:	O'Reilly Production Services	**Illustrator:**	Robert Romano

Revision History for the First Edition:

2011-09-23	First release
2012-03-16	Second release

See *http://oreilly.com/catalog/errata.csp?isbn=9781449306465* for release details.

ISBN: 978-1-449-30646-5

[LSI]

1331910292

Table of Contents

Preface

Almost every startup company in 2011 uses the word "social" in their business plans —although few actually know how to analyze and understand the social processes that can result in their firms' success or failure. If you are working in social media, social CRM, social marketing, organizational consulting, etc., you should read this book for insights on how social systems evolve and change, and how to detect what is going on.

Despite the title, the book is not *just* for startups. In fact, it is a "course-in-a-book", encapsulating nearly a semester's worth of theoretical and practical material—read it and you will know enough about social network analysis to be "dangerous". If you are a student in the field, we strongly encourage you to seek out and read every paper and book referred to in the footnotes. This will make you conversant in the classic literature of the field and enable you to confidently start your own research project.

If you are of a technical or computer science background, this book will introduce you to major sociological concepts and tie them back into things that can be programmed, and data that can be analyzed. If your background is social sciences or marketing, you may find some of the background material familiar, but at the same time will learn the quantitative and programmatic approaches to understanding humans in a social setting.

Prerequisites

This books is written to be accessible by a wide audience. We keep jargon to a minimum, and explain terms as they come along. However, there is a serious amount of technical content (as one expects from an O'Reilly book).

We expect you to be at least marginally conversant in Python—i.e., able to write your own scripts, understand the basic control structures and data structures of the language. If you are not yet there, we suggest starting with an online Python tutorial or Head First Python by Paul Barry (O'Reilly).

We do not cover in detail the process of harvesting data from Twitter, Facebook, and other data sources. Other books in O'Reilly's "Animal Guide" series provide ample coverage, including Twitter API: Up and Running by Kevin Makice, and Mining the Social Web by Matthew Russell.

Open-Source Tools

This book utilizes open-source Python libraries including NetworkX, NumPy, and MatPlotLib.

- NetworkX packages and documentation can be found at *http://networkx.lanl.gov/*.
  Aric A. Hagberg, Daniel A. Schult and Pieter J. Swart, "Exploring network structure, dynamics, and function using NetworkX", in *Proceedings of the 7th Python in Science Conference* (SciPy2008), eds. Gäel Varoquaux, Travis Vaught, and Jarrod Millman, pp. 11–15, Aug 2008.

- NumPy packages and documentation are at *http://numpy.scipy.org/*.
  Oliphant, Travis E. "Python for Scientific Computing". *Computing in Science & Engineering* 9(2007), 10-20 Ascher, D. et al. *Numerical Python*, tech. report UCRL-MA-128569, Lawrence Livermore National Laboratory, 2001.

- MatplotLib can be found at *http://matplotlib.sourceforge.net*.
  Hunter, J.D. "Matplotlib: A 2D Graphics Environment". *Computing in Science & Engineering* 9(2007), 90-95

Conventions Used in This Book

The following typographical conventions are used in this book:

Italic
> Indicates new terms, URLs, email addresses, filenames, and file extensions.

`Constant width`
> Used for program listings, as well as within paragraphs to refer to program elements such as variable or function names, databases, data types, environment variables, statements, and keywords.

`Constant width bold`
> Shows commands or other text that should be typed literally by the user.

`Constant width italic`
> Shows text that should be replaced with user-supplied values or by values determined by context.

This icon signifies a tip, suggestion, or general note.

 This icon indicates a warning or caution.

Using Code Examples

This book is here to help you get your job done. In general, you may use the code in this book in your programs and documentation. You do not need to contact us for permission unless you're reproducing a significant portion of the code. For example, writing a program that uses several chunks of code from this book does not require permission. Selling or distributing a CD-ROM of examples from O'Reilly books does require permission. Answering a question by citing this book and quoting example code does not require permission. Incorporating a significant amount of example code from this book into your product's documentation does require permission.

 All code, data, and examples can be downloaded from our GitHub repository at *https://github.com/maksim2042/SNABook*.

We appreciate, but do not require, attribution. An attribution usually includes the title, author, publisher, and ISBN. For example: "*Social Network Analysis for Startups* by Maksim Tsvetovat and Alexander Kouznetsov (O'Reilly). Copyright 2011 Maksim Tsvetovat and Alexander Kouznetsov, 978-1-449-30646-5."

If you feel your use of code examples falls outside fair use or the permission given above, feel free to contact us at *permissions@oreilly.com*.

Safari® Books Online

 Safari Books Online is an on-demand digital library that lets you easily search over 7,500 technology and creative reference books and videos to find the answers you need quickly.

With a subscription, you can read any page and watch any video from our library online. Read books on your cell phone and mobile devices. Access new titles before they are available for print, and get exclusive access to manuscripts in development and post feedback for the authors. Copy and paste code samples, organize your favorites, download chapters, bookmark key sections, create notes, print out pages, and benefit from tons of other time-saving features.

O'Reilly Media has uploaded this book to the Safari Books Online service. To have full digital access to this book and others on similar topics from O'Reilly and other publishers, sign up for free at *http://my.safaribooksonline.com*.

How to Contact Us

Please address comments and questions concerning this book to the publisher:

O'Reilly Media, Inc.
1005 Gravenstein Highway North
Sebastopol, CA 95472
800-998-9938 (in the United States or Canada)
707-829-0515 (international or local)
707-829-0104 (fax)

We have a web page for this book, where we list errata, examples, and any additional information. You can access this page at:

http://www.oreilly.com/catalog/0636920020424/

To comment or ask technical questions about this book, send email to:

bookquestions@oreilly.com

For more information about our books, courses, conferences, and news, see our website at *http://www.oreilly.com*.

Find us on Facebook: *http://facebook.com/oreilly*

Follow us on Twitter: *http://twitter.com/oreillymedia*

Watch us on YouTube: *http://www.youtube.com/oreillymedia*

Content Updates

March 16, 2012

Fixed typographical errors.

Thanks

Max Tsvetovat would like to thank his teachers, Sergei Fyodorovich Ivanov (High School #367, St. Petersburg, Russia), Maria Gini (University of Minnesota), and Kathleen Carley and Katya Sycara (Carnegie Mellon University), for putting up with an unruly student for so many years—and most importantly, for teaching me to think on my feet and to learn on my own. He thanks his family for their encouragement and patience during late night writing sessions (and specifically little David for sleeping through the night and letting Daddy work). Music by Miles Davis. Coffee by NorthSide Social. Wardrobe by...darn it, who am I kidding?

Alex Kouznetsov owes thanks to many friends, teachers, and colleagues who each did their part in shaping his path. He thanks his family for the support, and especially his wife Natalia for her active interest and taking care of life's logistics. Special thanks go to Nikolai Afanasievich Kolobov (Moscow Institute of Electronics and Mathematics) for demonstrating the joy of unorthodox thinking, scientific rigor, and a subsequent switch to natural sciences; and a longtime friend Javier Sanchez, for teaching me how to think critically and learn on my own, for fun and profit.

## CHAPTER 1

Introduction

"So...what do you do?"

"I'm a social network analysis researcher."

"Oh, so you play on Facebook and get paid for it?"

This dialogue occurs frighteningly often in the life of any SNA researcher. And the answer of "Yes, but it's much more than Facebook" does not cut it. In fact, SNA is an extremely versatile methodology that predates Twitter and Facebook by at least 30 years.

In a few words, Social Network Analysis (SNA) can be described as a "study of human relationships by means of graph theory." However, this sentence leaves a lot to be unpacked.

In a way, SNA is similar to many statistical methods. The fact that economists use regression analysis extensively doesn't mean that the technique is limited to the study of economics. Similarly, while studying the social media is a great way to apply SNA techniques—not only is the data easily available, but the opportunities for studying are numerous and lucrative. In fact, I am willing to bet that 9 out of 10 of my esteemed readers have picked up this book for this very reason.

Ten years ago, the field of social network analysis was a scientific backwater. We were the misfits, rejected from both mainstream sociology and mainstream computer science, applying strange mathematical techniques to strange sorts of data and coming up with pretty pictures that were very hard to read and results that made sense only within our narrow community. Social network data was difficult to gather and hard to come by (see Appendix A); most students in the field worked from a small standard set of datasets and rarely ventured out to build their own data. The advent of the Social Internet changed everything. Every day, Twitter generates more social-network data than our entire field possessed 10 years ago; every social media site provides an API for easy retrieval of data; many governments of the world are releasing data that lends itself to SNA techniques.

In this book, we will analyze social media data. We will harvest data from Twitter (Appendix A), from Facebook and LiveJournal. We will learn to recognize online communities, and study the anatomy of a viral video and a flashmob.

However, I will show that SNA can be applied in many different ways. In this book, we will look at the social media, but we will also look beyond social media. We shall study the relationships between companies through investment networks and through shared boards of directors. We will look inside an organization and discover how the social network around the water cooler and lunchroom affects the company's ability to perform—and how a company could shoot itself in the foot by ignoring this. We will look at campaign finance and discover how a single special-interest group can control the outcome of an entire election. We will explore the world of terrorists, revolutionaries, and radicals—from stories of the Khobar Towers bombing in 1998 and the 9/11 attacks, to the recent uprising in Egypt. We shall look at the anatomy of fads and trends—which are often mediated by Twitter and Facebook, but are offline phenomena by nature.

I will show you that network data is everywhere—you just need to learn to recognize and analyze it. And once you do, new insights and ideas shall follow.

Analyzing Relationships to Understand People and Groups

The science of Social Network Analysis (SNA) boils down to one central concept—our relationships, taken together, define who we are and how we act. Our personality, education, background, race, ethnicity—all interact with our pattern of relationships and leave indelible marks on it. Thus, by observing and studying these patterns we can answer many questions about our sociality.

What is a relationship? In an interpersonal context, it can be friendship, influence, affection, trust—or conversely, dislike, conflict, or many other things.

Binary and Valued Relationships

Relationships can be binary or valued: "Max follows Alex on Twitter" is a binary relationship while "Max retweeted 4 tweets from Alex" is valued. In the Twitter world, such relationships are easily quantified, but in the "softer" social world it's very hard to determine and quantify the quality of an interpersonal relationship.

A useful stand-in for strength of an interpersonal relationship is frequency of communication. Besides being objectively measurable, frequency of communication has been found by scientists to reflect accurately on the emotional content, and amount of influence in a relationship. This would, of course, not be true in many contexts (and you, my dear reader, are probably busy coming up with counterexamples right now)—but in many cases, for the lack of better data, frequency of communication works.

Symmetric and Asymmetric Relationships

It is easy to see that some relationships are asymmetric by nature. Teacher/student or boss/employee roles presume a directionality of a relationship, and do not allow for a symmetric tie back. Following on Twitter and LiveJournal is directional by definition —but a follow-back tie can exist, thus symmetrizing the relationship

Other relationships are symmetric. Facebook friends and LinkedIn connections require mutual confirmation—the software forces a symmetry even when the real human relationship is asymmetric.

In the real world, friendships and romantic relationships are asymmetric, as much as we would like them not to be that way. Hence, we struggle with unrequited love, one-sided friendships and other delusions of popularity. Given good data, we can study these phenomena using SNA—but such data would be very difficult to obtain and subject to self-reporting and other biases.

Multimode Relationships

Finally, we should mention that relationships can exist between actors of different types —Corporations employ People, Investors buy stock in Corporations, People possess Information and Resources, and so on. All of these ties are described as *bimodal* or *2-mode*—we will discuss them in detail in Chapter 5.

From Relationships to Networks—More Than Meets the Eye

If a traditional quantitative sociologist or econometrician got a hold of social network data, he would approach it as follows:

- What can we learn about the respondents? Is there any demographic data on them? Age, race, religion, income, education, location, and so on—any qualitative or quantitative variables that could possibly be measured.
- What kind of quantitative metrics can be derived from the network data? Most likely, these metrics would include various forms of centrality (see Chapter 3).
- What kind of quantitative or qualitative outcomes can be measured? That is, the ability to integrate into a society as a citizen, the likelihood of trying illegal drugs, etc.

Then he would build a multivariate regression model, controlling for some variables and linking some of the other variables to outcomes. This is a perfectly valid approach —in fact, this approach still gets a lot of mileage in the SNA conferences.

One of the traditional applications of this approach is the notion of *homophily* (Greek, meaning love of the similar)—or, loosely, the notion that "birds of a feather flock together." For example, it has been proposed that people of a similar age are more likely to be friends than people of different generations, or that people of the same race tend to associate together. While some of these conjectures ring true, they do not account for such things as the complexity of internal dynamics of social groupings between black teenagers in one high school class—where age, race, economic background, music preferences, etc., may all have a high degree of similarity, and yet emotions run the full spectrum of human conditions from love to rage.

However, we can do something that is remarkably different and, I dare say, better.

The standard statistical approach has one assumption—that of event independence, or a *Poisson process*.[1] In a Poisson process, every event can be treated as a completely independent occurrence, with no relationship to other events. Thus, we can compute probability of an event based on outside variables or characteristics—and as a result, come up with a decent model of reality. Of course, events are not always independent—in which case, Bayesian statistics can create chains of dependencies and compute the probabilities of macro-outcomes. Details of this are beyond the scope of this book, but can be found in a variety of sources.

In a social network, we intuitively know that there are no independent events. People form friendships and acquaintances through introduction—i.e., A meets B because A and B both know C. There are love triangles (which, in the view of homophily, should become more like a free-love commune!). There are long-range ties to unlikely others, on the basis of homophily.[2] And counter-examples multiply.

When we do SNA, we remove the independence assumption and treat all ties as potentially dependent on each other. This makes traditional statistical methods (e.g., regressions, or Markov Models) mathematically intractable on all but most trivial problems—but have no fear, we shall develop and deploy new methods that are just as powerful. We shall talk more about homophily in the context of information diffusion in "How Does Information Shape Networks (and Vice Versa)?" on page 116.

Social Networks vs. Link Analysis

Another cousin to SNA is Link Analysis (LI). Some of you may have used LI in business intelligence or law enforcement work, or seen it on TV. "Without a Trace" uses link analysis in every episode; "Numbers" and "Law and Order" resort to it on occasion.

Link analysis is in many ways similar to SNA—both talk about relationships in terms of nodes and edges (Figure 1-1) and both try to derive the idea of who is more important in a network by analyzing the whole network, not individual events.

---

1. *http://en.wikipedia.org/wiki/Poisson_process*

2. Yours truly is friends with both people on the radical left and radical right of the political spectrum, yet experiences little cognitive dissonance.

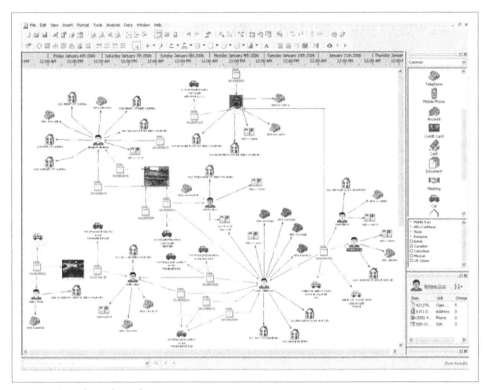

Figure 1-1. Link Analysis chart

However, LI allows for a mixing of different node and edge types in the same network —i.e, "**A** *gave* **$300** to **B** to *procure* **drugs** for **C**". In this example, **bold** words are nodes, or actors, and *italic* are actions, or edges. The problem is understanding on a quantitative level whether the act of giving money is different than the act of procuring drugs—and thus LI relies on human-level understanding of language and is qualitative in its pure form.

Most link analysis tools, including Analyst's Notebook and Palantir, include qualitative data gathering and tools for qualitative decision-making, and these are excellent and utilized widely in a number of communities. However, the application of quantitative metrics centrality measures is dangerous because mixing nodes and edges of different meanings (e.g., money and telephone calls) produces a result that is mathematically invalid. Unfortunately, this does not stop the software from computing these metrics. [3]

The proper way to address this is using multimode networks (which we discuss in Chapter 5), which is precisely what we are going to do.

3. Did I just make some enemies? I might live in Washington, DC, but I don't play politics with math. It's either right or wrong...sorry, guys.

The Power of Informal Networks

Let us start discussion of social network analysis with a little story.

ACME Consulting was an old auditing shop. Founded in the 1960s, it was a family-owned business for more than 25 years. The firm grew slowly and organically for many years, and was the owner's pride and joy. ACME's main business was accounting and auditing—serving a few select, reliable clients. In the mid-1990's, ACME succumbed to the lure of the information age, and added an IT department that built all of the infrastructure needed for running a "21st century operation"—but the core of the business was old-fashioned, with a nose-to-the-grindstone understanding of the paperwork and the numbers.

However, all good things must come to an end, and the owner, nearing his retirement years, decided to move to Boca Raton and embark on a new career of fly fishing and being a full-time grandfather. He didn't want to sell the business, and instead hired an outside CEO to run the company while the family remained nominally in control.

The org chart in Figure 1-2 shows how the CEO (Conrad) saw his company. The auditors and the IT groups formed their own divisions, of about 100 people each (the org chart below is greatly simplified). Separate was a "secretarial pool"—a group whose sole responsibility was dealing with mountains of paperwork that the firm handled for clients. In a way, this was a vestige of the "Mad Men" world—some of the older auditors still referred to the secretaries as "girls," despite the fact that many of them were in their 50s. The departments bickered with each other over resources and requirements, problem resolution took far too long and required too many meetings, and cost the company many billable hours.

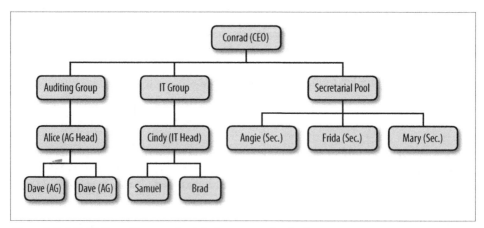

Figure 1-2. ACME Consulting org chart (before reorganization)

This way of doing business didn't sit well with CEO Conrad, a young graduate of a prestigious business school. He wanted to build a modern, client-oriented, responsive organization. Shortly after his arrival, ACME was reorganized. Every client account was now assigned an "engagement manager" and was served by a cross-functional team that handled all of the work, from server installation to filing tax returns. The secretarial pool was dissolved, and its functions were distributed to client sites. You can see the new org chart in Figure 1-3.

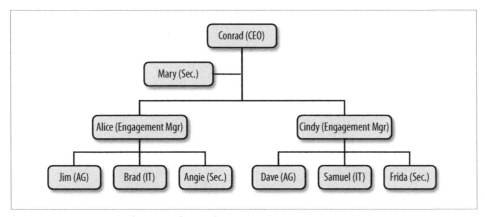

Figure 1-3. ACME Consulting org chart (after reorganization)

On the surface, the change was good. The project teams finally got to know their clients; finance and IT people finally talked to each other and realized that they were not actually born on different planets, routine problems got resolved in hours instead of weeks. Customers were happier. But under the surface, trouble was brewing.

Over time, Conrad noticed that each of the project teams spent more and more time "firefighting"—fixing previous mistakes. Tracking the kinds of mistakes, he realized that many of them had to do with improper forms being filed with the government, misplaced documents, and other concerns that we would call "routine paperwork"— things that used to be handled by the secretarial pool. The final straw was a major mistake that nearly landed ACME on the front page of the Wall Street Journal. Then, Conrad did what any manager in this situation would do—he hired a consultant.

Let us now trace what the consultant did, and repeat after him.

If you have not yet installed the tools of our trade—Python and NetworkX—I will now refer you to Appendix B for installation instructions. Once you have installed all the necessary software and libraries, please open your Terminal and clone the GitHub repository (*http://www.github.com/maksim2042/SNABook*), and "cd" to the working directory. At the prompt (%), type python to launch the Python command line interpreter. You will be given a prompt (>>>) at which you can type and execute individual Python statements:

```
% python
>>> import networkx as net
>>> import matplotlib.pyplot as plot
```

```
>>> orgchart=net.read_pajek("ACME_orgchart.net")
>>> net.draw(orgchart)
```

You should now see something similar to the picture in Figure 1-4. The hierarchical layout of ACME is evident with Conrad in the center, flanked by project teams led by Cindy and Alice.

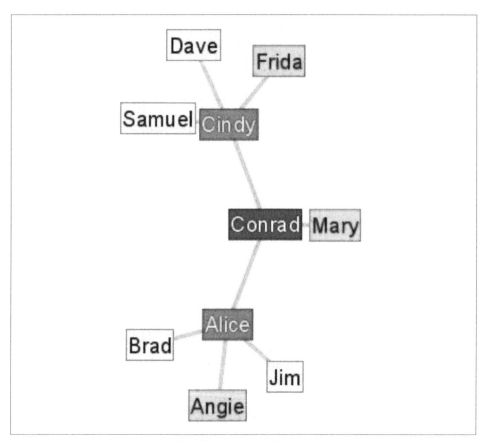

Figure 1-4. ACME Consulting org chart (formal network)

The consultant was not content with seeing the formal structure of the organization, and instead proceeded to talk to the employees about the company and the way things were done "in the old days" and after arrival of the new CEO.

The questions he asked were simple: *"Who gives you advice?"*, *"Who do you trust?"*, and *"Who do you socialize with after work?"*.

The results were nothing short of astounding—at least to the CEO. The real network of ACME was not even close to its organizational chart, and it revealed the crucial mistake made by Conrad (see Figure 1-5). Let us reproduce this figure:

```
>>> advice = net.load_pajek("ACME_advice.net")
>>> net.draw(advice)
```

In the informal network, the most trusted person was not the CEO (who was still seen as an interloper), nor one of the managers—but Frida, one of the secretaries from the "old girls club." A closer examination showed that Frida was one of the oldest employees of the firm, and was regarded as a mentor by almost everyone else. After more than 20 years with ACME, Frida had accumulated both factual and tacit knowledge that made the firm stable. However, in Conrad's reorganization, she had been moved to an offsite client team, and her advice became unavailable on a day-to-day basis.

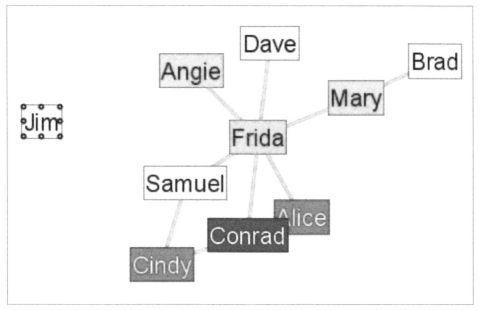

Figure 1-5. ACME Consulting Org. Chart—Informal Network

This story has a happy ending. Frida was promoted and stayed at the headquarters as a trusted advisor, training the younger employees—and the company rapidly recovered.

This story serves to demonstrate that informal networks matter, more than many managers would like to admit. Every organization has information bottlenecks, rumor mills, competing cliques and other potential problems that only Social Network Analysis can detect.

I tell this story every time I teach Social Networks to various audiences—from graduate students to government officials. On more then one occasion, people have asked me "So how do you stop informal networks from happening?". It is in fact impossible to do so.

Terrorists and Revolutionaries: The Power of Social Networks

Informal social networks emerge in the harshest conditions, despite all efforts to prevent them. Just like the Internet, social networks tend to route around damaged connections and restore communications.

Social Networks in Prison

In the infamous Butyrka prison in Moscow, the authorities strictly forbid communication between cells. The wall are too thick to allow yelling from cell to cell, there is no common exercise yard, and every attempt at communication detected by authorities is punished by solitary confinement. One cannot imagine a harsher environment for maintenance of an informal social network. Nevertheless, over the years an intra-prison mail system ("malyava") has evolved that allows letters and small packages (Figure 1-6) to be moved from cell to cell undetected.

Figure 1-6. A prison network "packet" delivered on a rope through the window. The address on the packet contains the cell number that it came from, and the destination.

It works essentially as a packet-switching network. A system of point-to-point links moves "packets" on long loops of string (called "roads") through the windows and over the outside walls (packages must be small enough to fit through the bars). If an outside "road" is not available, a package may be pulled through the sewer pipes after being waterproofed with a plastic bag. The packets are then either received and read, or routed on to the next cell—until they reach the intended recipient. The "roads" are disrupted whenever authorities find them—but can be reestablished in a matter of hours. Over time, as prisoners are moved to other cells, shipped to serve the rest of their sentence in Siberia, or released, the network adapts and is continuously optimized for reliability.

This system even allows for broadcast messages (e.g., "such-and-such has been snitching to the authorities; whoever sees him next should punish him") and runs on a strict set of social norms ("thieves' law") enforced by the inmates with extreme violence. [4]

---

4. Unfortunately, data on informal prison networks is not readily available. We know they exist and how they function in many ways—but empirical collection of this data is all but impossible. In English, the best source is the "Gulag Archipelago" by Alexander Solzhenitsin.

While the "malyava" system works well within an individual prison, contact must be maintained with other prisons (e.g., for prisoners shipped to jails in Siberia). This is much more difficult—the process of moving a prisoner to a faraway prison camp involves many searches that make shipping a letter or a package with a courier nearly impossible. Thus, important information gets communicated by word-of-mouth through trusted people—usually professional criminals with many prison terms behind them. The information migrates from one medium to the next and, if needed, is disseminated along the way.

This, for example, ensures that an informer cannot hide from the "thieves' law" no matter where he goes—information about his deeds will eventually reach any prison camp he might be sent to, guaranteeing a violent outcome. The informal network also serves more peaceful purposes, letting experienced criminals consult with younger ones in the profession, resolving property disputes, and establishing a firm set of norms of behavior that is remarkably civilized for the population.

One curious aspect is that the Soviet government originally encouraged (or pretended not to notice) the development of this code of behavior—as it helped the authorities keep the Gulag system under control, and marginalize political prisoners to the advantage of the professional thieves.

Informal Networks in Terrorist Cells

The Al Qaeda manual of operations states that a cell preparing an attack should be small, not more than 6 members. The members of the cell live together in a safe-house and only leave it to go on reconnaissance or supply missions, and maintain little or no ties to the community. Only the cell leader possesses information about contacts and supply routes within the larger organization—which minimizes the risk of exposure should some of the operatives (frequently young and badly trained) be caught.

The manual is available from the US Department of Justice or the Federation of American Scientists at *http://www.fas.org/irp/world/para/ manualpart1_1.pdf*. Please be careful when downloading on corporate or government networks as possession of this document could be misinterpreted.

Let us walk a little bit through the logic of this network:

- Sequestering a small group of people inside a safe-house ensures that the operatives will bond with each other to the exclusion of their own families or outside connections. These bonds act as a positive feedback loop, helping extremist ideology to be accepted and amplified within the group. We will discuss these amplification loops in Chapter 4.

- Keeping the group small, while an obvious limitation to the size and complexity of the operation, allows everyone in the group to constantly monitor everyone else, and not leave a hiding place where a single individual may communicate with the outside world and give away the location and plans of the cell.

- Keeping a single connection to the outside world through the cell leader allows the organization to control (as well as filter and distort) all information that goes in and out of the safe-house, making the operatives fully dependent on the organization for survival.

I used the operations manual and a number of other sources to build a model of social network structure similar to that of a terrorist network.[5] One such simulated structure is shown in Figure 1-7. In this network, two separate groups of operatives are preparing two separate attacks—a group on the right headed by *Agent 6* and a larger group on the left headed by *Agent 36*.

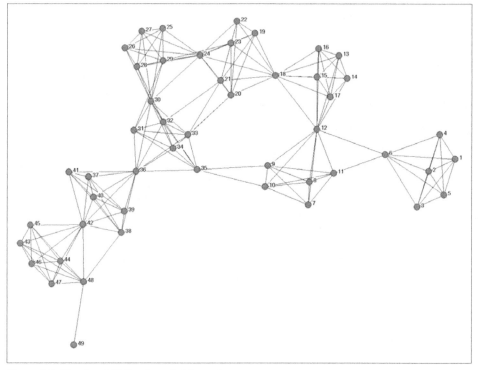

Figure 1-7. Simulated Al Qaeda-style Network

5. Tsvetovat, M. and K. M. Carley. "Structural Knowledge and Success of Anti-Terrorist Activity: The Downside of Structural Equivalence." *Journal of Social Structure* (*http://www.cmu.edu/joss/*) 6 (2005).

Intuitively, if a law enforcement or military officer is shown this picture, he would recognize agents 6 and 36 as leaders—or important in some way—and propose that they be targeted for an offensive operation (whether it is an arrest or a drone strike). In fact, this is one of the most common ways social network analysis is applied in the counter-terrorism community. The leader of the cell is indeed a weak spot and his removal presents a significant problem for the operatives—but, in fact, the informal network of the terrorist organization is capable of quickly recovering from such an attack.

Figure 1-8 shows this adaptation process after an attack. In step 3, *Agent 36* is removed, leaving a large group of operatives without a connection to the main body of the organization. However, each of the agents inside the cell possesses some informal knowledge of other individuals in the organizations—perhaps through training camps, or family ties. After the attack on Agent 36, a chaotic frenzy of informal connection attempts ensues; most of these informal connections do not succeed. However, once a successful connection is made, the entire group of operatives is reconnected to the main organization, largely undoing the effects of the drone strike. In my simulation, this process takes approximately a week.

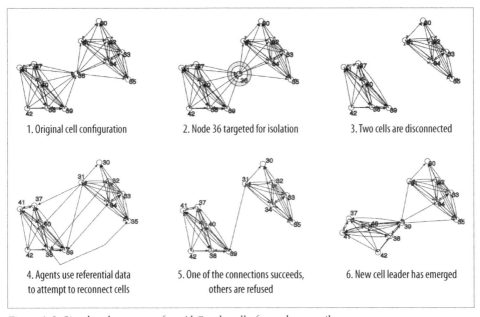

Figure 1-8. Simulated recovery of an Al Qaeda cell after a drone strike

The Revolution Will Be Tweeted

The revolutions that shook the Arab world in the winter of 2011 are frequently described as "Twitter Revolutions". They are not the first political uprisings mediated by online social networks—the first successful one was in Moldova in 2009;[6] one also cannot underestimate the role of Twitter in the suppressed Iranian uprising. However, the revolutions in Tunisia and Egypt presented the biggest and most public challenge to the existing world order.

Social Media and Social Networks

How did social media become so powerful? How did it graduate from sharing pictures of cats to toppling governments?

The answer lies in the social media's ability to maintain and amplify *weak ties*. Weak ties are defined as social connections between people that require little or no emotional attachment, some agreement on basic terms (but low overall similarity), low frequency of communication—in short, they require little or no personal time and energy to maintain—yet are extremely powerful. Mark Granovetter, in his groundbreaking paper,[7] shows how weak ties in an interpersonal network (not mediated by Twitter or Facebook) can carry information across vast distances both physical and social (in terms of income, class and attitudes). Low emotional content of such ties allows people to hold very different opinions on many topics without engaging in a conflict; low frequency of communication means that the two people are usually desynchronized in terms of what information they receive and when. Thus, when two people do communicate across a weak tie, the information that passes through it is usually novel, and comes from a different point of view. Granovetter showed that weak ties are extremely important in a job search; people that one was strongly tied to tended not to possess any novel information about job openings, but people across weak ties had access to very different information and could make far-ranging connections.

With all of the power of a weak tie, its probability of being useful is fairly low—while the cost of maintaining the weak tie is non-zero (in terms of time investment). Furthermore, the human species seems to have a biological limitation to the number of people they can maintain a tie to. Robin Dunbar states that our cognitive limit is, in fact, *only 150*.[8] The variance of this number is quite high, as we all know gregarious individuals who seem to know literally everybody—but secondary evidence supports that a qualitative shift occurs in organizations, villages, military units, etc., when they

---

6. You can read about Moldova's Twitter Revolution online at *http://neteffect.foreignpolicy.com/posts/2009/04/07/moldovas_twitter_revolution*.

7. Granovetter, Mark. "Strength Of Weak Ties, A Network Theory Revisited." *Sociological Theory* 1 (1983), 201-233.

8. Hill, R. A. and Dunbar, R.,"Social network size in humans." *Human Nature* 14 (2003), 53-72.

grow beyond 150 individuals (i.e., beyond the number that everyone could keep in their heads). Nevertheless, no matter what the real number is, the theory still holds.

Why do we talk about this in context of Twitter? Social networking sites help minimize the time and cost of maintenance of a large number of weak ties (it is much easier to update your Twitter status and read a stream of updates than to call every one of your friends daily and ask how they're doing)—and thus increasing the potential number and reach of these weak ties. Moreover, the one-sided "follow" relationships of Twitter allow for non-reciprocal relationships and broadcast communication—thus Twitter can quickly turn ordinary people into celebrities. They just have to be at the right place at the right time.

Take the example of *@ReallyVirtual*, an IT consultant who accidentally live-tweeted the raid against Osama bin Laden's compound in Abottabad. The morning of the attack, he had a small number of followers (measured in the 100s)—which shot into tens of thousands as major media outlets found out about him and publicized his Twitter account. Currently, he has close to 100,000 followers—but does it really mean that he has 100,000 relationships? Not really—these are weak ties that have been precipitated by a single event, a Warholian 15-minutes-of-fame moment.

Egyptian Revolution and Twitter

Now let's return to the revolution in Egypt, and analyze the Twitter traffic over February 24-25, 2011. Figure 1-9 shows the dynamics of Twitter posts from Tahrir Square on the eve of Mubarak's resignation. While it is obvious that every newsworthy event culminates with a spike in Twitter activity, it is also interesting to observe that major events also include a run-up in number of tweets in the hours preceding the event—reflecting the rumors and "buzz" of the crowd expecting something major to happen.

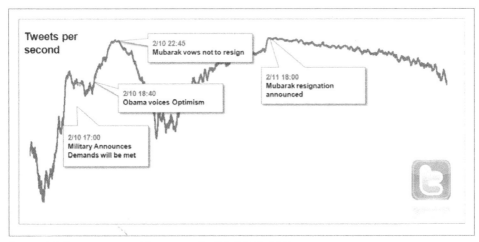

Figure 1-9. News events and Tweet rate for Feb 24-25, 2011

However, let us dive a little deeper into the social networks that helped Egyptian revolution to happen.

We at DeepMile Networks [9] collected the data on the Egyptian revolution as the events were unfolding. We were mainly interested in mapping out the process by which people in the streets of Cairo were exchanging information and influencing each other.

We consider a retweet to be the basic unit of influence on Twitter. It represents information that has been received, internalized, and passed on to others. If we follow the history of every message, video, tweet, etc., in the online universe, we'll find that by far the largest majority of messages get no reaction whatsoever—and a very small number "go viral"—that is, get diffused to a large number of people.

The picture in Figure 1-10 shows a portion of the retweet network that we have observed.[10] A link between two people in the network represents that some retweeting has occurred between the two people; we find that over time people tend to retweet from others that they trust—so, collected over time, this network becomes a proxy for trying to understand who trusts whom. A number of clusters of dense retweeting activity has formed in the network, with some of the clusters having several hundred members passing information to each other. Some of the clusters are geographically distributed (some are in Egypt, others are in France and the US), others represent different topics—anything from movement of security forces to searching for a toilet in the vicinity of the Tahrir Square.

In tracking the retweets from Tahrir Square, we found that a small number of people were able to generate disproportionately larger response to their tweets than anyone else. This did not depend on the number of followers that a person had—rather, the biggest determinant of being influential is whether a person is embedded in a dense cluster of like-minded people.

Compare the two networks in Figure 1-11. These networks were extracted from the large network dataset that we collected and are centered on two prominent individuals that have voiced their opinions on the Egyptian Revolution. On the left is Wael Ghonim, a Google employee that became one of the central figures over the course of events. At the time of the revolution, he had 80,000 followers—however, his tweets generated 3200 reactions each. To compare, we have found the person with the largest number of followers in the network—Justin Bieber. With his cadre of 7.5 million followers, he generated only 300 reactions per tweet.

---

9. DeepMile Networks (*http://www.deepmile.com*) is a highly specialized management and technology consulting firm that delivers cutting edge solutions to the advertising and national security communities.

10. An abridged dataset can be downloaded from *https://github.com/maksim2042/SNABook/tree/master/chapter1*.

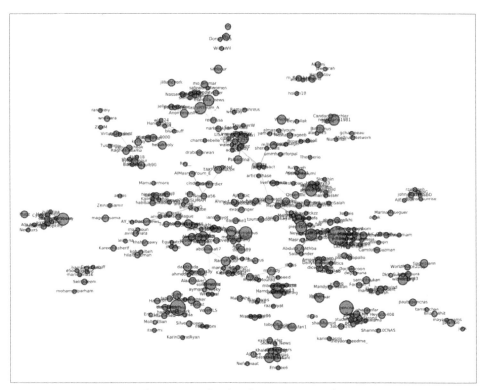

Figure 1-10. Retweet network on topics related to the Egyptian Revolution

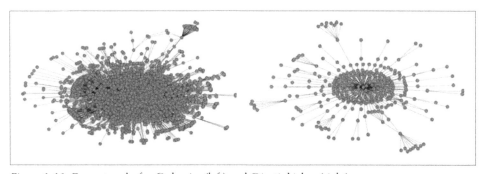

Figure 1-11. Ego networks for @ghonim (left) and @justinbieber (right)

Following the same reasoning, we drilled further into the data and realized that a large number of individuals that were deeply embedded into the dense communities and clusters were responsible for generating and spreading the information. The conclusion of our study was that the revolution was not broadcast by celebrity or well-known voices—the messages found a resonance chamber inside the dense clusters populated by everyday people.

In short, this is a praise for the network "middle class"—not the celebrities, not the inactive lurkers—but people who only have a medium number of followers, but actively maintain their networks by investing time into them by following up on and responding to messages. Together in a dense cluster, this middle class formed a formidable force in Tahrir Square.

We shall spend more time on information diffusion and "viral phenomena" in Chapter 6, after we have established a solid base of tools and understanding to undertake influence analysis.

## CHAPTER 2

Graph Theory—A Quick Introduction

What Is a Graph?

A graph is, arguably, one of the most ubiquitous mathematical abstractions. Even if you have never encountered this mathematical concept before, you have most likely worked with graphs before. A project plan is a graph; a circuit diagram is a graph; dependencies between files in a software project are graph.

In this book, we shall mostly deal with one type of graph—social graphs or social networks. A social network is simply a collection of sentences that describe relationships, in the following way:

```
Alice ----likes-----> Bob
(noun)   (verb)    (noun)
```

The simple phrase above is a basic unit of social network analysis called a *dyad*. Every dyad denotes a single relationship—an *edge* in traditional graph theory (although I use the words *edge* and *relationship* interchangeably). The nouns in the phrase represent people involved in the relationship—these are called *vertices* (plural of *vertex*) or *nodes* in the mathematical literature (we shall use *nodes* exclusively).

In social network analysis, nodes have a type. Each node could represent a person, organization, a blog posting, a hashtag, etc. If a graph contains nodes of only one type, it's called a *1-mode* graph. If it contains relationships between two types, it's *bimodal* or *2-mode*. We can also have multimodal graphs.

We shall start our exploration of social networks with 1-mode graphs—i.e., graphs that link people to people, organizations to organizations, words to words, and so on. We will explore 2-mode graphs in Chapter 5, and multimode networks in Chapter 6.

Now let's pay some attention to the verb that signifies the content (*semantics*) of a relationship, something that could be as simple as a series of phone call timestamps, or so complex as be only describable in poetry. Interpreting poetry of relationships is still—and perhaps will forever be—an unsolved problem (until we reach Kurzweil's Singularity)—so we are going to concern ourselves with a simpler interpretation of content.

We will (at least for now) make the following hard assumption: All edges in the networks we analyze will use a *single, consistent verb*. This, of course, is highly limited, incapable of describing even a simple high-school love triangle:

```
Alice likes Bob very much.
Bob and Carol study together.
Carol fights with Alice after school.
```

However, it is a highly practical assumption, especially for social media applications, where the semantics of a relationship is firmly set by the software developers. After all, every "follow" on Twitter is the same, and so is every "friend" on Facebook.

 Curiously, every social media site has chosen to interpret the word "friend" in a completely different manner. So, we cannot mix Facebook, Twitter, and LiveJournal data without a semantic translation. We shall address some of these issues in Appendix A.

In some instances, edges can have a numeric value. Sociologists would frequently use something called a Likert scale, for example:

```
0. Don't know
1. Strongly dislike
2. Dislike
3. Neither dislike nor like
4. Like
5. Strongly like
```

However, the Likert scale has a limited usefulness to social networks. If one administered a survey based on this scale, it would come out heavily skewed towards values 3,4,5—people tend to under- or misreport negative relationships[1] and there are not enough gradations (or relevant examples) to distinguish "like" from "strongly like".

---

1. Krackhardt, David. "Cognitive Social Structures." *Social Networks* 9 (1987) 109-134.

The following scale (designed by David Krackhardt)[2] is better. Instead of a subjective "do you like person X" questions, it asks a more objective "How often do you communicate with X?":

```
0. Never
1. At most once a year
2. At most once a month
3. At most once a week
4. At most once a day
5. Many times a day
```

It turns out that frequency of communication maps pretty cleanly on the subjective "friendship" or "liking" scale. After all, if you dislike someone, would you talk to them more often than you have to?

An interesting feature of this scale is that it minimizes self-reporting errors. It's very easy to remember if one talked, say, once a month or once a year. Finally, this scale can be objectively measured, by considering things like email timestamps or blog post replies.

Adjacency Matrices

The basic way to represent a social network mathematically is a matrix:

```
  A B C D E
A 0 1 0 1 1
B 1 0 0 1 0
C 0 0 0 1 1
D 1 1 1 0 0
E 1 0 1 0 0
```

A "1" in cell AB, for example, means that there's a relationship (edge) between nodes A and B. In case of a valued graph (using the frequency scale above), the matrix would look like this:

```
  A B C D E
A 0 2 0 5 5
B 2 0 0 1 0
C 0 0 0 3 4
D 5 1 3 0 0
E 5 0 4 0 0
```

The major downside of adjacency matrices is that zeros (i.e., "no edge" cells) take the same amount of memory as the other cells. In real social networks, there are a lot of zero cells—in fact, over 90% of cells would be zeros. The ratio of non-zero cells to zero cells is called *density*. Most online social networks have density of 0.1% or less; in fact, the larger a social network is, the lower its density will be.

---

2. Also described in Krackhardt's article, "Cognitive Social Structures".

Edge-Lists and Adjacency Lists

The solution to the density problem above is to represent networks as *edge-lists*:

```
from to value
A    B  2
A    D  5
A    E  5
B    A  2
B    D  1
C    D  3
C    E  4
D    A  5
D    B  1
D    C  3
E    A  5
E    C  4
```

or, in Python:

```
>>> edges = {{'A','B',2}, {'A','D',5}....etc....}
```

This representation takes significantly less space for large and sparse (i.e., low-density) networks; it also maps perfectly to SQL database tables (you can read more about SQL in ""Medium Data": Database Representation" on page 142) and text-based file formats such as *.net* (learn more about on file formats in ""Small Data"—Flat File Representations" on page 139). The disadvantage of this structure is that it only allows iterating over the edges, but not fast search or traversal through the graph.

We can do even better, using a format called *adjacency list*:

```
from   edges
A      (B 2),(D 5),(E 5)
......
```

Or, in Python:

```
>>> edges = {'A':{'B':2, 'D':5, 'E':5}, 'B':{'A':2, 'D':1}}
```

The adjacency list above is based on Python *dict* data structures (Appendix B). Searching is fast, adding and removing nodes and edges is easy—however, this structure is awkward to parse from text files or write to databases.

 In practice, we usually use edge list for persistent storage, and adjacency lists for internal data representation. Adjacency matrices are difficult to manipulate in practice, especially with large networks, but are useful in understanding many of the algorithms in the rest of this book.

7 Bridges of Königsberg

A classic illustration of graph traversal is that of the Seven Bridges of Königsberg—a little puzzle dating back to the time of Immanuel Kant. Situated on a small strip of land sandwiched between Poland and Lithuania, Königsberg (now Kaliningrad) was founded in the 13th century and, until 1945, remained an important (although small) city in German culture, home to both Kant and Leonhard Euler, one of the greatest mathematicians of the 18th century.

The city was set on the Pregel River, and included two large islands that were connected to each other and to the mainland by seven bridges. The 16th century plan of the city (Figure 2-1) shows these bridges; only 5 of them survived the bombardments of World War II, and most of the buildings on the central island have been demolished (Figure 2-2).

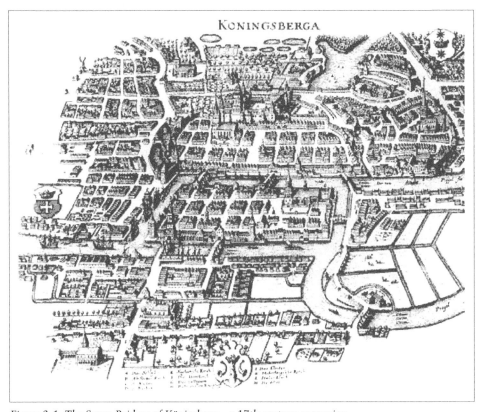

Figure 2-1. The Seven Bridges of Königsberg—a 17th century engraving

Figure 2-2. The Five Bridges of Kaliningrad—a modern view. This is all that remains after World War II, but Euler's theorem still holds

An apocryphal story is that Immanuel Kant was well-known in the city for taking long walks so regular that people could set their clocks by him. He was endlessly frustrated by the fact that on his return home he had to pass over the same bridge as he took in the beginning of his walk (being a rather pedantic sort, I guess), so he posed the problem over dinner to his friend Leonhard Euler. In process, he inadvertently helped invent a new branch of mathematics.

Euler formulated this problem as a graph (Figure 2-3); the two banks of the river and the islands were represented as graph *nodes* and the bridges as *edges*. Thus, a path through the city becomes a path (or a traversal) through the graph. The question of the bridges, thus, is formulated as follows: is it possible to traverse a graph without repeating any edges (but possibly repeating nodes) and returning to the starting point.

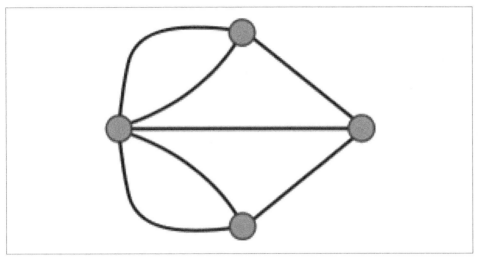

Figure 2-3. The Seven Bridges of Königsberg—a graphical representation

Euler proved that this is indeed not possible—no path (i.e., a walk that does not repeat an edge) is possible through this graph.

Try it yourself on the graph—you will realize why it caused Kant enough frustration that he lobbied the mayor to build an eighth bridge.

Graph Traversals and Distances

Webs are meant to be spidered or crawled, links are meant to be hopped—walking the structure of a network is at the root of many powerful techniques and metrics—some of which will be presented later in this book.

When we talk about "walking" or "crawling" the graph, we mean an algorithm that, from some starting point, follows links to its neighbors, and in turn the neighbors' neighbors, and so on—in some predetermined order. Some walk algorithms are designed to find the shortest path from point A to point B; others attempt to walk the entire graph to understand or sample its structure—but all have common properties.

Let us use the following terminology:

- A *leaf node* is a node with only one incoming connection.
- A *child node* is a node connected to a starting node; the starting node then is a *parent node*.
- Two *child nodes* of a single *parent node* are *sibling nodes*.

Let us create a simple graph with 10 nodes and 18 edges (Figure 2-4):

```
>>> import networkx.generators.small
>>> g = networkx.generators.small.krackhardt_kite_graph()
>>> g.number_of_edges()
18
>>> g.number_of_nodes()
10
>>> g.adjacency_list()
[[1, 2, 3, 5], [0, 3, 4, 6], [0, 3, 5], [0, 1, 2, 4, 5, 6], [1, 3, 6],
 [0, 2, 3, 6, 7], [1, 3, 4, 5, 7], [8, 5, 6], [9, 7], [8]]
>>> g.edges()
[(0, 1), (0, 2), (0, 3), (0, 5), (1, 3), (1, 4), (1, 6), (2, 3), (2, 5),
 (3, 4), (3, 5), (3, 6), (4, 6), (5, 6), (5, 7), (6, 7), (7, 8), (8, 9)]
```

We can also get the familiar adjacency dictionary:

```
>>> dict((x, g.neighbors(x)) for x in g.nodes())
{0: [1, 2, 3, 5], 1: [0, 3, 4, 6], 2: [0, 3, 5], 3: [0, 1, 2, 4, 5, 6],
4: [1, 3, 6],  5: [0, 2, 3, 6, 7], 6: [1, 3, 4, 5, 7], 7: [8, 5, 6],
8: [9, 7], 9: [8]}
```

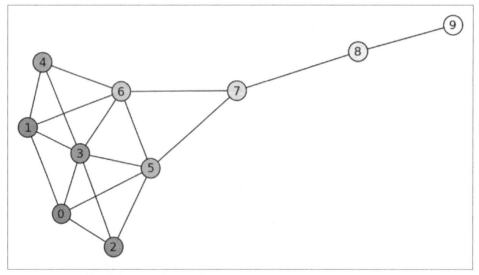

Figure 2-4. Krackhardt kite social network

This looks like regular Python but it is IPython with *%doctest_mode* enabled. With IPython we can type *object?* to get details about it, including any docstrings.

```
>>> networkx.generators.small.krackhardt_kite_graph?
Type:           function
Base Class:     <type 'function'>
String Form:    <function krackhardt_kite_graph at 0xa1367d4>
Namespace:      Interactive
File:           /usr/lib/python2.6/site-packages/networkx-1.3-py2.6.egg/networkx/
generators/small.py
Definition:     networkx.generators.small.krackhardt_kite_graph(create_using=None)
Docstring:
    Return the Krackhardt Kite Social Network.

    A 10 actor social network introduced by David Krackhardt
    to illustrate: degree, betweenness, centrality, closeness, etc.
    The traditional labeling is:
    Andre=1, Beverley=2, Carol=3, Diane=4,
    Ed=5, Fernando=6, Garth=7, Heather=8, Ike=9, Jane=10.
```

For out traversals we will also need to import the traversal module:

```
>>> from networkx.algorithms import traversal
```

Depth-First Traversal

 We are using NetworkX version 1.5. Some of the methods mentioned here may not be available in the earlier versions, so be sure to upgrade.

Depth-first search (DFS) is an uninformed search that systematically traverses nodes until it finds its goal. In the context of a tree, DFS involves descending down a child's child, iteratively, and then backtracking and turning to each of its siblings—in other words, it prefers to go deep before going broad. In a graph there are no children or siblings, only neighbors. However, DFS can produce a *spanning tree* of the nodes it has visited.

Here is the DFS algorithm, simplistically described:

- Start at some node n
- Mark n as visited
- For each neighbor n_i of n where n_i has not been visited,
    — recursively apply DFS to node n_i

You may also wish to keep track of the edges that led to newly discovered nodes (*discovery edges*) and the edges used for backtracking (*back edge*). These edges together form the spanning tree: a representation of the algorithm's path through the graph.

We describe this algorithm recursively, there is also an iterative form using a stack to maintain visited nodes. To a computer scientist each is an implicit version of the other.

Implementation

A list of nodes in the order they were visited:

```
def DFS_nodes(graph, node, visited=[]):
    visited.append(node)
    for neighbor in graph[node]:
        if not neighbor in visited:
            DFS_nodes(graph, neighbor, visited)
    return visited
```

A list of edges in the order they were traversed. This does not include back edges; neither does the NetworkX implementation below:

```
def DFS_edges(graph, node, visited=[], edges=[]):
    visited.append(node)
    for ni in graph[node]:
        if not ni in visited:
            edges.append((node, ni))
            DFS_edges(graph, ni, visited, edges)
    return edges
```

Let us try them on our graph (see Figure 2-5):

```
>>> DFS_nodes(g, 0)
[0, 1, 3, 2, 5, 6, 4, 7, 8, 9, 0]
>>> DFS_edges(g, 0)
[(0, 1), (1, 3), (3, 2), (2, 5), (5, 6), (6, 4), (6, 7), (7, 8), (8, 9)]
```

DFS with NetworkX

NetworkX provides a DFS implementation by D. Eppstein (you can see it in all its glory at *http://www.ics.uci.edu/~eppstein/PADS/DFS.py*):

```
>>> edges = traversal.dfs_edges(g)
>>> edges
<generator object dfs_edges at 0x99a42ac>
```

The traversal returns a *generator* object, a Python construct for lazy evaluation. When used in a for loop it behaves just like a sequence. We can "unwrap" a generator into a real list:

```
>>> list(edges)
[(0, 1), (1, 3), (3, 2), (2, 5), (5, 6), (6, 4), (6, 7), (7, 8), (8, 9)]
```

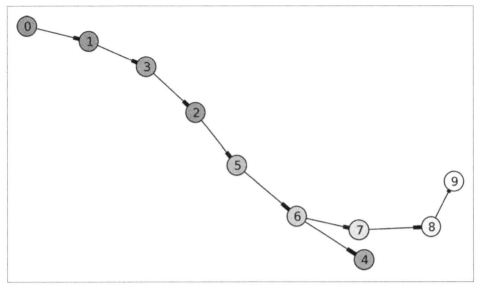

Figure 2-5. DFS tree of Krackhardt kite social network

By default, a DFS traversal starts at the first known node, in this case, node 0. It can be any other node.

We can get a more conventional tree view with a successor dictionary:

```
>>> traversal.dfs_successors(g)
{0: [1], 1: [3], 2: [5], 3: [2], 5: [6], 6: [4, 7], 7: [8], 8: [9]}
>>> # also, predecessor are available -- a view of the tree upside down:
>>> traversal.dfs_predecessors(g)
{1: 0, 2: 3, 3: 1, 4: 6, 5: 2, 6: 5, 7: 6, 8: 7, 9: 8}
>>> # remember, this is all just lists and dictionaries!
>>> traversal.dfs_successors(g)[3]
[2]
>>> traversal.dfs_successors(g)[6]
[4, 7]
```

Finally, we can produce a directed graph representing the DFS traversal:

```
>>> tree = traversal.dfs_tree(g)
>>> tree
<networkx.classes.digraph.DiGraph object at 0x99a558c>
>>> tree.successors(0)
[1]
>>> tree.succ
{0: {1: {}}, 1: {3: {}}, 2: {5: {}}, 3: {2: {}}, 4: {}, 5: {6: {}}, 6: {4: {}, 7: {}},
 7: {8: {}}, 8: {9: {}}, 9: {}}
```

Breadth-First Traversal

Breadth-first traversal or search (BFS) is the opposite of DFS: it visits all of the immediate neighbors first and only then proceeds to their neighbors.

Algorithm

BFS and DFS are very similar, the only difference is the order in which they traverse encountered nodes. DFS will explore a new neighbor node immediately as it sees it whereas BFS must store each neighbor until it has seen them all, and only then descend down each one. Therefore, while DFS is happy with a stack to hold its "nodes to be explored," BFS requires a queue. As a consequence, there is no natural recursive form for BFS. Here is the algorithm:

- Start with node n
- Create queue Q
- Mark n as visited
- Enqueue n onto Q
- While Q is not empty:
    - Dequeue n' from Q
    - For each neighbor n_i of n' that has not been visited,
        - mark n_i as visited
        - enqueue n_i onto Q

 Replacing the queue with a stack turns BFS into DFS!

BFS with NetworkX

The interface is similar to DFS, with one distinction: a starting node must be specified.

```
>>> edges = traversal.bfs_edges(g, 0)
>>> list(edges)
[(0, 1), (0, 2), (0, 3), (0, 5), (1, 4), (1, 6), (5, 7), (7, 8), (8, 9)]
>>> tree = traversal.bfs_tree(g, 0)
>>> tree
<networkx.classes.digraph.DiGraph object at 0x99b266c>
```

The difference between DFS and BFS traversal trees is clearly visible (Figure 2-5 and Figure 2-6):

```
>>> traversal.bfs_successors(g, 0)
{0: [1, 2, 3, 5], 1: [4, 6], 5: [7], 8: [9], 7: [8]}
>>> traversal.dfs_successors(g, 0)
{0: [1], 1: [3], 2: [5], 3: [2], 5: [6], 6: [4, 7], 7: [8], 8: [9]}
```

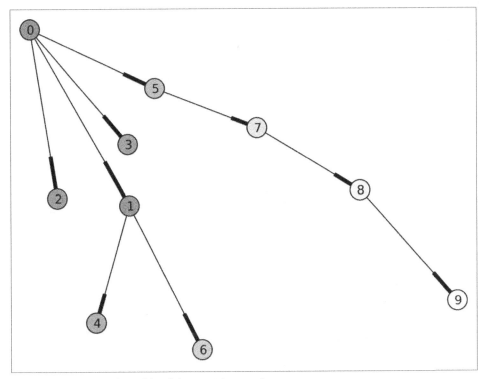

Figure 2-6. BFS tree of Krackhardt kite social network

Paths and Walks

A *walk* is an alternating sequence of nodes and edges that connect them (obviously, when there are no more than one edge connecting each pair of nodes, the sequence of nodes fully describes a walk). A walk is *open* if the starting and ending nodes are different and *closed* otherwise. The *length* of the walk is the number of edges.

A *path* is an open *simple* (where no node is crossed twice) walk. A closed simple walk is a *cycle*. Formally a path can have length 0, whereas a cycle cannot (Figure 2-7).

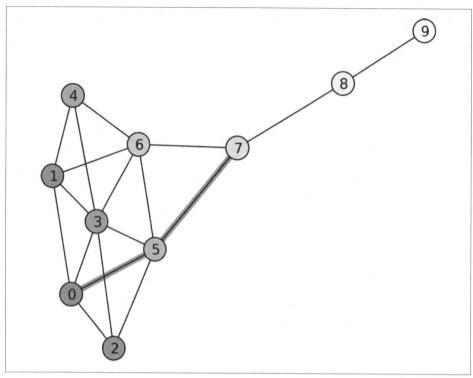

Figure 2-7. Shortest path between 0 and 7

Paths and cycles are essential to understanding the structure of graphs and quantifying that with machines. NetworkX provides a number of path algorithms:

```
>>> from networkx import algorithms
>>> algorithms.shortest_path(g,0,5)
[0, 5]
>>> algorithms.shortest_path(g,0,7)
[0, 5, 7]
>>> algorithms.average_shortest_path_length(g)
1.9777777777777779
```

For those feeling adventurous, we can even list the shortest paths in a graph:

```
>>> algorithms.all_pairs_shortest_path(g)
{0: {0: [0], 1: [0, 1], 2: [0, 2], 3: [0, 3], 4: [0, 1, 4], 5: [0, 5], 6: [0, 1, 6],
7: [0, 5, 7],
 8: [0, 5, 7, 8], 9: [0, 5, 7, 8, 9]}, 1: {0: [1, 0], 1: [1], 2: [1, 0, 2], 3: [1, 3],
4: [1, 4],
 5: [1, 0, 5], 6: [1, 6], 7: [1, 6, 7], 8: [1, 6, 7, 8], 9: [1, 6, 7, 8, 9]}, 2: {0:
[2, 0],
 1: [2, 0, 1], 2: [2], 3: [2, 3], 4: [2, 3, 4], 5: [2, 5], 6: [2, 3, 6], 7: [2, 5, 7],
 8: [2, 5, 7, 8], 9: [2, 5, 7, 8, 9]},
 ...
```

Or, all shortest paths from a specific node:

```
>>> algorithms.all_pairs_shortest_path(g)[5]
{0: [5, 0], 1: [5, 0, 1], 2: [5, 2], 3: [5, 3], 4: [5, 3, 4], 5: [5], 6: [5, 6], 7:
[5, 7], 8: [5, 7, 8], 9: [5, 7, 8, 9]}
```

For more algorithms, please consult the documentation: *http://networkx.lanl.gov/refer ence/algorithms.shortest_paths.html*.

Dijkstra's Algorithm

A special mention goes to a graph search algorithm published by Edsger Dijkstra in 1959.[3] For a given vertex it finds the lowest cost path to all other vertices, where "cost" is determined by summing edge weights. In graphs where edge weights correspond to distance (in unweighted graphs the weights are assumed to be one) the found path is the shortest. The algorithm can also determine the lowest cost path between two given vertices:

```
>>> algorithms.dijkstra_path(g, 1, 5)
[1, 0, 5]
>>> algorithms.dijkstra_predecessor_and_distance(g, 1, 5)
({0: [1], 1: [], 2: [0, 3], 3: [1], 4: [1], 5: [0, 3, 6], 6: [1], 7: [6],
   8: [7], 9: [8]}, {0: 1, 1: 0, 2: 2, 3: 1, 4: 1, 5: 2, 6: 1, 7: 2, 8: 3, 9: 4})
```

We can actually compare the shortest path algorithms with relative ease. First, we will need node pairs:

```
>>> import itertools
>>> g.nodes()
[0, 1, 2, 3, 4, 5, 6, 7, 8, 9]
>>> list(itertools.combinations(g.nodes(), 2))
[(0, 1), (0, 2), (0, 3), (0, 4), (0, 5), (0, 6), (0, 7), (0, 8), (0, 9), (1, 2),
 (1, 3), (1, 4), (1, 5), (1, 6), (1, 7), (1, 8), (1, 9), (2, 3), (2, 4), (2, 5),
 (2, 6), (2, 7), (2, 8), (2, 9), (3, 4), (3, 5), (3, 6), (3, 7), (3, 8), (3, 9),
 (4, 5), (4, 6), (4, 7), (4, 8), (4, 9), (5, 6), (5, 7), (5, 8), (5, 9), (6, 7),
 (6, 8), (6, 9), (7, 8), (7, 9), (8, 9)]
```

Note that because our graph is undirected we don't need to look at reverse paths, but even this may be a little too much. For brevity, we can limit the node space to, say, first 4 nodes, using Python's array slicing syntax:

```
>>> nn = g.nodes()
>>> nn
[0, 1, 2, 3, 4, 5, 6, 7, 8, 9]
>>> nn[:4]
[0, 1, 2, 3]
>>> pairs = list(itertools.combinations(nn[:4], 2))
>>> pairs
[(0, 1), (0, 2), (0, 3), (1, 2), (1, 3), (2, 3)]
```

3. Dijkstra, E. W. "A note on two problems in connexion with graphs". *Numerische Mathematik* 1 (1959) 269–271

Using another Python technique, argument array expansion, we can look at them side by side:

```
>>> for pair in itertools.combinations(nn[:8], 2):
    print algorithms.shortest_path(g, *pair), algorithms.dijkstra_path(g, *pair)
...
[0, 1] [0, 1]
[0, 2] [0, 2]
[0, 3] [0, 3]
[0, 1, 4] [0, 1, 4]
[0, 5] [0, 5]
[0, 1, 6] [0, 1, 6]
[0, 5, 7] [0, 5, 7]
[1, 0, 2] [1, 0, 2]
...
```

Oh well—they are the same. But what about weights? Not a problem; we can throw some random weights at the graph and see what happens. We do this by constructing a list of node-node-weight triples from the list of node pairs. For our eyes' sakes let us use integer weights between 1 and 10:

```
>>> from random import choice
>>> new_edges = [x + (choice(range(10)),) for x in ee]
>>> new_edges
[(0, 1, 1), (0, 2, 9), (0, 3, 3),
(0, 5, 5), (1, 3, 5), (1, 4, 8),
(1, 6, 7), (2, 3, 6), (2, 5, 4),
(3, 4, 3), (3, 5, 0), (3, 6, 0),
(4, 6, 2), (5, 6, 1), (5, 7, 6),
(6, 7, 3), (7, 8, 4), (8, 9, 9)]
>>> g.clear()
>>> g.add_weighted_edges_from(new_edges)
```

Now we can compare the paths again:

```
>>> for pair in itertools.combinations(nn[:8], 2):
    print algorithms.shortest_path(g, *pair), algorithms.dijkstra_path(g, *pair)
...
[0, 1] [0, 1]
[0, 2] [0, 3, 5, 2]
[0, 3] [0, 3]
[0, 1, 4] [0, 3, 6, 4]
[0, 5] [0, 3, 5]
[0, 1, 6] [0, 3, 6]
[0, 5, 7] [0, 3, 6, 7]
[1, 0, 2] [1, 0, 3, 5, 2]
[1, 3] [1, 0, 3]
[1, 4] [1, 0, 3, 6, 4]
...
```

Graph Distance

We have been referring to the notion of *distance* between nodes of a graph. Graph distance is an abstraction of a walk—we ignore the process of walking and simply look at how close or far the nodes are (this is not to be confused with *closeness*, which is a measure of node's *centrality*; more on that later). In other words, we may not care to go from A to B, but knowing the distances can tell us a great deal about the graph.

Graph distance can be measured in a number of ways:

Shortest path (unweighted graph)
> The simplest measure of distance: simply the number of edges that one must walk over from A to B.

Cost-based shortest path (weighted graph)
> In a *weighted* graph, every edge has an associated value, called *weight*. This value could, for example, represent the physical distance between two points on a topographic map. Naturally, the distance from A to B will be the sum of distances between the intermediate points. Provided we can only travel along the edges, the choice for the shortest path becomes obvious—it's the one with the least combined distance, but not necessarily the fewest nodes. Often we give this weight-as-a-distance value the more general term "*cost*," meaning it will cost us this many CPU cycles/hops/hours/etc., to travel the path.

Euclidean distance
> Euclidean distance is based on similarity of nodes. This similarity comes from the already-familiar adjacency matrix. More specifically, each node is treated as a point in Euclidean space, whose coordinates are given by a row (or column) of the adjacency matrix. The distance between two points in that space is proportional to the number of common neighbors shared between the nodes.

If you are concerned with the possibility of there being more than three coordinates to a point in space, do not be alarmed! The distance metric is still the root of the sum of squares of individual coordinate deltas, regardless of the number of dimensions. In computer science, this happens all the time.

Euclidean distance is also called "vector similarity," and is the basis for Vector Space Retrieval model...more on this later.

Graph Diameter

A graph's diameter is the largest number of vertices that must be traversed in order to travel from one vertex to another (paths that backtrack, detour, or loop are excluded from consideration). For example, the graph in Figure 2-8 has diameter 4.

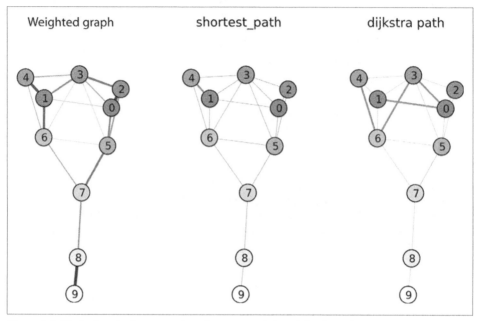

Figure 2-8. Nodes 1 to 4: shortest path vs. low-cost path in weighted graph

Why This Matters

Graph distance is a way to quantitatively analyze a graph. In social networks, where nodes communicate to their neighbors and relay messages between them, graph distance gives us an indication of how information is likely to propagate. Knowing that, we can begin measuring the *reach* of a network participant and assess his *influence*:

Unweighted graph
>   In an unweighted graph, distance is proportional to the ability of information to travel from Alice to Bob. That is, with all things being equal, Bob is less likely to hear something Alice said the further he is from her. This influences the formation of dense subnetworks, such as cliques (see "Cliques" on page 79).

Weighted graph
>   If we weighted the graph with the frequencies of individual communications (that we measured, for instance) then the distance would tell us how quickly can information spread from Alice to Bob. For more on information diffusion, see Chapter 6.

Euclidean distances

Nodes with short Euclidean distances have similar connections to the network and therefore may have similar or equivalent roles. We can further group nodes by their relative distance and begin to identify *clusters* (see "Hierarchical Clustering" on page 81).

6 Degrees of Separation is a Myth!

Almost everyone has heard of the notion of 6 degrees of separation. There was even a romantic comedy by that name.

The conventional wisdom goes like this: *there are no more than six connections between any two people on this planet.* This makes some sense on an intuitive level. After all, in our lives we accumulate connections, however weak or temporary, that link us to far-away lands. Max (your faithful author) is equally connected (by 2 or 3 degrees of separation) to a major Hollywood star, President Obama, a convicted Russian spy and a group of Kenyan farmers—and that's just a small subset carefully picked to astonish you.

It makes sense mathematically—if, on average, every person has 150 friends or acquaintances, then the number of people within 6 degrees of separation is 150^6, or roughly 11 trillion people, many orders of magnitude more than the overall number of people in the world. This number is computed assuming that there's no overlap—that your friends are not friends with each other. In real networks, this overlap factor can be quite high—but not high enough to bring the overall number down.

However, this is still a myth.

Let us go back in time to 1969. Psychologist Stanley Milgram (known for his daring experimental techniques, including the infamous "Milgram Experiment") sends out approximately 300 letters to various randomly picked addresses in Nebraska and Kansas. Each of the letters included instructions to try to get the letter delivered back to Boston through a chain of acquaintances—without resorting to looking up the address directly (which, in 1969, would have posed a serious library research challenge). Along with the letter were pre-addressed postcards that each of the nodes in the chain should mail to help track the progress of the letter.

Of the 300 letters sent, only 64 arrived, with the *average* chain length of 5.5. Average, not maximum! Combine this with a very small number of letters that have actually arrived and we have a number of inaccuracies. The maximum path length in the world is still not very long (perhaps 20 or so), due to a very interesting phenomenon.

Small World Networks

Let us imagine a lattice network (Figure 2-9)—a network where every node is connected to a few of its neighbors, in a very regular fashion. A path from one side of this network to another may be quite long (in this "toy problem," it's 5). Then, let us perturb the network by deleting some edges and replacing them with random edges. Having replaced 5 out of 17 edges, the diameter of the graph fell to 3, without significantly affecting the shape of the graph. At the same time, the original local structure of the graph remains—nodes that were neighbors before are still neighbors.

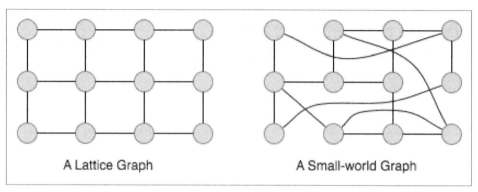

Figure 2-9. A lattice network and its preturbation

These kind of networks are called "small world networks"—they keep a local neighborhood structure but allow a small number of ties to reach far away. The prevailing argument in the community is that small world network-like shapes dominate the social network landscape. These networks consist of dense communities or neighborhoods that are loosely connected by *boundary spanners* (or, to link to Malcolm Gladwell's terminology, *Connectors*).

In the next chapter we will work to identify the communities, and find who these boundary spanners are.

CHAPTER 3

Centrality, Power, and Bottlenecks

In the previous chapter we have spent a fair bit of time talking about abstract concepts of graph theory. In this chapter, we shall return back to earth and start using them to analyze real social networks. We'll take a sample dataset from the social media blogging site LiveJournal.com—specifically a group of very vocal Russian expatriates—and try to learn about their community using SNA metrics.

The first set of metrics that we approach is one called "centrality". People new to the field often learn about degree centrality without realizing that it's just one of a family of metrics that can be used together or separately. In this chapter we'll explore the four most popular metrics, and learn to visualize and combine them.

But first, let's get acquainted with the data.

Sample Data: The Russians are Coming!

LiveJournal is a lively blogging site that is very popular in Russia and Eastern Europe. It currently serves close to 38 million blogs, most of them in languages other than English. The underlying server software is open-source, and presents a simple API and a generous policy for data mining and robots. (See *http://www.livejournal.com/bots/*.)

We are going to perform a data gathering protocol called Snowball Sampling (see Appendix A) and obtain a dataset that is suitable for further analysis.

Get Oriented in Python and NetworkX

If you have not yet installed Python and the NetworkX environment, please refer to Appendix B.

Now, let us get oriented with Python and NetworkX. Start Python, then import the NetworkX library and the UrlLib library (we'll need it shortly):

```
% python
>>> import networkx as net
>>> import urllib
```

NetworkX operates with graph data structures—which can be generated programmatically, created from information you fetch from online sources, or read from files or databases. Let us first make a simple graph (Figure 3-1) by hand:

```
>>> g=net.Graph()          #create a blank graph
>>> g.add_edge('a','b')   #insert an edge into the graph; nodes will be inserted
automatically
>>> g.add_edge('b','c')
>>> g.add_edge('c','a')
>>> net.draw(g)            #draw the graph like on <<fig_triple>>
```

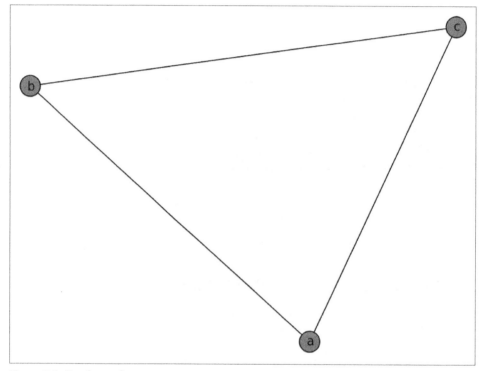

Figure 3-1. Simple graph

You can also print out or manipulate the nodes and edges of the graph as lists:

```
>>>> g.nodes()
['a','b','c']
>>>> g.edges()
[('a', 'c'), ('a', 'b'), ('c', 'b')]
```

A graph data structure in NetworkX is just like a Python *dict*—everything can be looked up nearly instantaneously, one just has to know the key:

```
>>> g.node['a']
{}
>>> g.node['a']['size']=1
>>> g.node['a']
{'size' : 1}
```

Nodes and edges can store arbitrary dicts of attributes, and any other type of rich data:

```
>>> g['a']  #returns a dict of neighbors and edge weights
{'b': {}, 'c': {}}

>>> g['a']['b'] #returns the attributes of the edge A->B
{}
>>> g['a']['b']['weight']=1 #sets an attribute of the edge
>>> g['a']['b']
{'weight' : 1}
```

Many of the metrics also return a dict, with node IDs as keys and metrics as values.

It's *dicts all the way down*!

Read Nodes and Edges from LiveJournal

We are going to use the LiveJournal data mining API to retrieve the data; we will use URLLib to fetch the data and parse it. LiveJournal exposes a simple text API; let's test it with CURL on the command line by fetching the list of friends of a user named *valerois*. This code:

```
% curl http://www.livejournal.com/misc/fdata.bml?user=valerois
```

returns:

```
# Note: Polite data miners cache on their end.  Impolite ones get banned.
> bagira
> evka
> angerona
> yelya
...(list truncated)...
< ponka
< marinka
```

Each line constitutes an edge between the source (*valerois*) and target (*bagira*, etc). The first character of the line denotes direction (< means "bagira connects to valerois"; > is the opposite).

The function below fetches a list of friends from the API, walks through the lines in the response and creates edges:

```
def read_lj_friends(g, name):
    # fetch the friend-list from LiveJournal
    response=urllib.urlopen('http://www.livejournal.com/misc/fdata.bml?user='+name)
```

```
# walk through the lines in the response and add each one as an edge in a network
for line in response.readlines():
    #Comments in the response start with a '#'
    if line.startswith('#'): continue

    # the format is "< name" (incoming) or "> name" (outgoing)
    #make sure that we don't have an empty line
    parts=line.split()
    if len(parts)==0: continue

    #add the edge to the network
    if parts[0]=='<':
        g.add_edge(parts[1],name)
    else:
        g.add_edge(name,parts[1])
```

The function takes two arguments—a graph object that the function will fill in with
nodes and edges, and a string "seed"—the username of the person whose friendship
network should be searched. Run this function against a sample username (*valerois*)
and draw it to produce a picture similar to Figure 3-2:

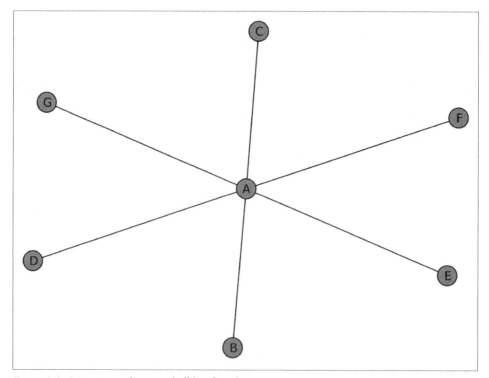

Figure 3-2. A LiveJournal user and all her friends

```
>>> g=net.Graph()
>>> read_lj_friends(g,'valerois')
>>> len(g)  #count the number of nodes returned
226
>>> net.draw(g)
```

Snowball Sampling

We will discuss network sampling and data collection at length in Appendix A, but right now we need some data, and we need it fast. We'll start with a simple algorithm called "Snowball Sampling" (also known in sociology as *chain sampling* or *respondent-driven sampling*). [1]

Roughly, snowball sampling works like a pyramid scheme—data provided by each respondent is used to recruit new respondents, or:

```
* Start with a central node
* Obtain friends of the central node
* For every one of the friends:
*       sample friends of the friends
*       For every friend-of-friend
*              sample friends-of-friends-of-friends...
* etc...
```

This translates into a recursive routine, not entirely unlike the breadth-first search[2] of a graph. One concern with snowball sampling is the explosion of data that it can deliver. Imagine that every person on LiveJournal, on average, has 100 friends. Thus, he might have 10,000 friends-of-friends, and a million friends-of-friends. Fortunately, real social networks usually have a lot of overlap—100 friends translates to 2000-3000 friends-of-friends.

A further reason for limiting depth of search is a human limit of perception of social networks—known in the field as a Horizon of Observability. [3] We are pretty good at knowing who our friends are (average accuracy is ~ 70%), but our knowledge of the social network drops off rapidly. Only 30% of friends-of-friends are known, and there is almost no knowledge about friends-of-friends-of-friends.

In practice, we usually limit the depth of the search to two (friends-of-friends) or three levels (friends-of-friends-of-friends)—this provides a fairly complete picture of the network surrounding central actors, without pulling out too much of the peripheral data.

1. Goodman, L.A. "Snowball sampling". *Annals of Mathematical Statistics* 32 (1961), 148–170. *http://dx.doi.org/10.1214%2Faoms%2F1177705148*

2. Russel, S. and P. Norvig. *Artificial Intelligence, a modern approach*. Prentice Hall, 2003.

3. Friedkin, N.E. "Horizons of Observability and Limits of Informal Control in Organizations." *Social Forces* 62 (1983), 54-77.

The procedure below is a Python implementation of a snowball sampling for Live-Journal. The function takes 2 required parameters—a network object into which new nodes and edges will be inserted, and name of a central node. The optional parameter max_depth is initially set at 1—this will just sample the immediate neighbors of the central node. Use it for testing—then increase to 2 or 3 to get a larger dataset:

```
def snowball_sampling(g, center, max_depth=1, current_depth=0, taboo_list=[]):

    print center, current_depth, max_depth, taboo_list
    if current_depth==max_depth:
        # if we have reached the depth limit of the search, return.
        print 'out of depth'
        return taboo_list
    if center in taboo_list:
        #we've been here before -- return right away
        return taboo_list
    else:
        taboo_list.append(center) # we shall never return to the same node

    read_lj_friends(g, center) # call LiveJournal API and get data for a node.

    for node in g.neighbors(center):
        # Iterate through all friends of the central node, call snowball_sampling
recursively
        taboo_list=snowball_sampling(g, node, current_depth=current_depth+1,
max_depth=max_depth, taboo_list=taboo_list)

    return taboo_list
```

Call this function like this:

```
>>> g=net.Graph()
>>> snowball_sampling(g,'kozel_na_sakse')
```

Saving and Loading a Sample Dataset from a File

Since data harvesting can take time—especially with snowball sampling—let's not forget to save the data. We are going to use a Pajek[4] format—a simple text-based format that has been a lingua franca for exchanging network data:

```
>>> net.write_pajek(g,'lj_friends.net')
```

Once the data has been saved, one can open this file in almost any other SNA package.

---

4. The .net file format was first used by a venerable software package called *Pajek* (which means "spider" in Slovenian); the software comes from University of Ljubljana.

Centrality

One of the first approaches of analyzing social networks is to measure power, influence, or other individual characteristics of people (based on their connection patterns(. However, the community disagrees quite a bit about what power and influence mean, and which connection patterns correspond to various manifestations of these qualities. In this section, we will survey a number of methods of measuring power and influence (called "centrality" in jargon), and discuss their relative merits and usefulness.

Who Is More Important in this Network?

One of the first questions one asks when looking at a social network is *who is more important in this network?*, or *who has the power?*. In the introduction (see "The Power of Informal Networks" on page 9), we showed a network ruled by a powerful (yet largely invisible) secretary; similar insights can follow from a variety of network metrics that are all described under the heading of *centrality*.

However, there is little agreement on what centrality actually means. In my practice the first answer is usually "it depends." It depends on the data—what does it mean that two people are connected? Did they just "friend each other" on a social networking site —or do they have a deeper connection? It depends on whether the links mean information exchange, or responsibility (as in the case of organizational networks). It depends on the understanding of power and influence that is desired as an output.

In this chapter, we will explore the four classic centrality metrics and interpret them using the Russian LiveJournal data that we collected in the previous section.

Find the "Celebrities"

Every community has its own Paris Hiltons and Lady Gagas—people who are significantly more popular than others. There are usually very few of them, and they are orders of magnitude more popular then everyone else. The first and simplest metric that we use will help us find these local celebrities.

This metric is called *degree centrality*.

A *node degree* is simply the number of connections that a node has. On Twitter, it's the number of followers; on Facebook, it's the number of friends; and on Reddit, it could be interpreted as the number of upvotes ("link karma").

A quick inspection would tell us that person A in the star network (Figure 3-2) is in an exceptional structural position. All lines of communication lead to him, and all communications on the network must go through him. Thus we may be tempted to conclude that A is powerful merely by nature of his position.

But is he really? This largely depends on the nature of the links and nature of the relationships. Furthermore, in real-world social networks, pure star configurations like this are exceptionally rare. Most likely, lateral ties between, for example, B and C (or any others) exist, but for some reason were not included in the dataset.

According to Scott Adams, the creator of Dilbert, the power a person holds in the organization is inversely proportional to the number of keys on his keyring. A janitor has keys to every office, and no power. The CEO does not need a key: people always open the door for him. But then, of course, comes the Almighty Janitor:

> In the unlikely event I ever become president of a company, my first order of business will be to promote the janitor to executive vice president. Then I'll call him into my office and say "All right, Herb, I want you to tell me what's going on in the company. Care for a drink before we begin? I think I have a bottle of Scotch around here someplace." "Lower left drawer of your desk," Herb will reply, "Right behind your box of El Puffo cigars, which, I might add, are excellent."
>
> — Patrick McManus, The Good Samaritan Strikes Again

However, degree is a useful metric in messy network data such as the one we have obtained from Live Journal. And an easy start.

Let us turn to this data and apply degree centrality to a real-world network.

Degree centrality in the LiveJournal network

First, let us load the sample data. If you have finished running the snowball data collection ("Snowball Sampling" on page 43), you can skip this step and proceed directly to the analysis:

```
>>> g=net.read_pajek('russians.net')
>>> len(g)
87250
```

This is a very large network, so we are not going to attempt to visualize it just yet. However, we will use a degree metric to find the core of the network.

Degree is returned as a Python *map*—a set of name-value pairs linking node names to the degree value:

```
# compute degree
>>> deg=net.degree(g)
>>> deg['valerois']
232
>>> min(deg.values())
1
>>> max(deg.values())
4691
```

```
### This function returns a sorted degree list -- useful for celebrity-spotting
>>> def sorted_map(map):
...     ms = sorted(map.iteritems(), key=lambda (k,v): (-v,k))
...     return ms
...
>>> ds=sorted_map(d)

### Top 10 people in the list
>>> ds[0:9]
[('borisakunin', 4691), ('doctor_liza', 3046), ('tareeva', 2970), ('cheger', 2887),
('karial', 2717), ('snorapp', 2707), ('masha_koroleva', 2683), ('elladkin', 2616),
('samoleg', 2597)]
```

The top user in this dataset is indeed a celebrity—he is a best-selling writer of Russian detective novels as well as a regular fixture on the blogging scene. *doctor_liza* is the head of a charity that raises money and awareness in the blogosphere to provide medical care to Russia's poor and homeless. *tareeva* is a writer and an opposition politician. Everyone on the top ten list is an interesting personality in one way or another, from food writers to award-winning animation artists.

As you can see, the range between minimum and maximum degree is enormous. Let us see how the degree is distributed. This will require that you have installed the *matplotlib* package:

```
>>> import matplotlib.pyplot as plot
>>> h=plot.hist(deg.values(),100)       ## display a histogram of node degrees
                                        ## in 100 bins
>>> plot.loglog(h[1][1:],h[0])          ## plot the same histogram in Log-Log space
```

Figures 3-3 and 3-4 show the distribution of degrees in the Russian network. Most of the nodes have degree of 1, while a small minority compose a dense core of highly interconnected nodes. Looking at the histogram, one would be tempted to conclude that the network is scale-free.[5] However, let us momentarily revert to the way we have collected data.

The snowball method has a predefined maximum depth—in this case, max_depth=2. Thus, we know *about* many of the nodes—but we have not actually visited them to find how many neighbors they have. These nodes are *undersampled* and represent a fuzzy boundary of the network, rather than real pendant nodes. Since our goal is to find the core of popular users in the network, let's remove them for now:

5. Barabási, Albert-László. *Linked: How Everything Is Connected to Everything Else and What it Means for Business, Science, and Everyday Life.* Perseus Books: 2002

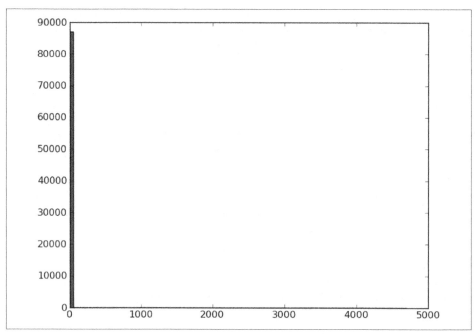

Figure 3-3. Degree histogram

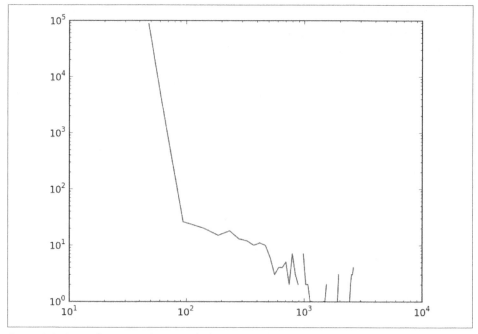

Figure 3-4. Degree histogram (LogLog Plot)

```
# return a new graph object that contains the network with pendant and
# isolated nodes removed
def trim_degrees(g, degree=1):
  g2=g.copy()
  d=net.degree(g2)
  for n in g2.nodes():
      if d[n]<=degree: g2.remove_node(n)
  return g2


>>> core=trim_degrees(g)
>>> len(core)
25905
```

However, this still leaves more nodes than can be readily visualized. Let us repeat the trimming operation until we have a smaller set:

```
>>> core2=trim_degrees(g,degree=2)
>>> len(core2)
11743

>>> core3=trim_degrees(g,degree=3)
>>> len(core3)
6373
....
....
>>> core10=trim_degrees(g,degree=10)
>>> len(core10)
619

>>> net.draw(core10)
```

The resulting picture depicts a dense core where no further structure can be distinguished—the "dreaded hairball" network (Figure 3-5). What this shows is that our Russian network consists of a *single* core and a periphery. The other common configuration for online social networks is that of multiple cores loosely connected to each other. In this case, each of the cores may be capable of developing its own subculture, jargon, celebrities, and so on. We shall spend more time discussing multicore networks in Chapter 4.

Find the Gossipmongers

The *ego*'s[6] ability to get information from and send information to others largely depends on the distance between it and the rest of the network. As I mentioned in "Snowball Sampling" on page 43, the *horizon of observability*—that is, the ability to see into the network—is about 2 levels, meaning that *ego* has almost no insight into what is happening 3 or more steps away. Ability to move information from one side of

---

6. From here on out, *ego* refers to a central node in any calculation, while *alter* refers to any of the other nodes connected to *ego*.

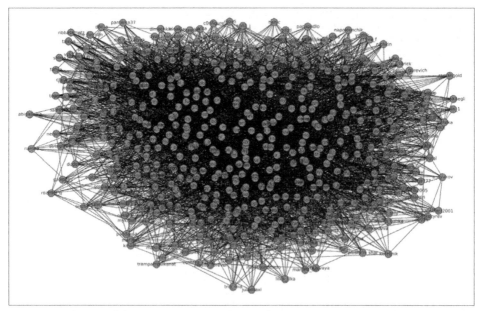

Figure 3-5. The core of the Russian LiveJournal network

the network to another (i.e., gossip) is an important step towards establishing a shared perception of the world—whether it has to do with someone's choice of outfits at a party or the formation of a political movement.

Thus, distance to others (or the inverse of it, closeness) can define a person's role in the network. This principle is at the root of the *closeness centrality* metric—the next centrality concept we will explore.

The calculation of closeness centrality is computationally expensive:

1. Compute the shortest path between every pair of nodes using Dijkstra's algorithm, and store these distances in a table.

2. For every node:

    a. Compute average distance to all other nodes

    b. Divide by maximum distance

    c. Closeness = 1 divided by average distance

The result is a number between 0 and 1, where higher numbers mean greater closeness (lower average distance). On our sample data, this can be computed as follows:

```
#We use the core graph because calculations on the entire 81000-node graph
#can take over an hour
>>> c=net.closeness_centrality(core10)

#sort the results using a function from previous section
>>> cs=sorted_map(c)
```

```
#top-10 gossipers
>>> cs[:10]
[('azbukivedi', 0.6155378486055777), ('valerois', 0.61370407149950346),
('bagira', 0.58969465648854957), ('karial', 0.57381615598885793),
('kpoxa_e', 0.57222222222222219), ('yelya', 0.53692441355343179),
('kirulya', 0.53645833333333337), ('angerona', 0.53506493506493502),
('borisakunin', 0.53184165232358005), ('snorapp', 0.53001715265866212)]
```

As we see, this list is fairly different from the high-degree individuals. Most of the members of the top ten are not celebrities or professional bloggers (with the exception of *borisakunin* and *snorapp* at numbers 9 and 10, both of whom are well-known writers). They are everyday individuals, many of them living in the United States. I will not mention names, but I know many of them personally.

Why do they have such high closeness centrality? Perhaps it has to do with the time and effort they invest in blogging and commenting on others' posts—building up a rapport with people one comment at a time. Rather than a means for promoting the latest book, or a professional activity, hanging out on the LiveJournal blogs is a way of life for them, for better or for worse.

As Figure 3-6 shows, the closeness centrality is not so heavily skewed. A few individuals still form the "long tail"—but the rest align to a bell curve at the low end of the spectrum. This shows that despite being a fairly dense network, the core of the LiveJournal network has local subsets that are more than two steps away from each other—that is, there are parts of the network core that are entirely invisible to the other individuals within the core.

Find the Communication Bottlenecks and/or Community Bridges

Betweenness centrality is based on the assumption that an individual may gain power if he presides over a communication bottleneck. In Figure 3-7, node *D* is clearly in a position of some power—all communications between nodes A,B and C; and nodes E, F, and G have to come through D. The bottleneck position can be precarious, however —it also translates to a considerable amount of stress. We will discuss the source of this stress in more detail later, in "The "Forbidden Triad" and Structural Holes" on page 72.

Betweenness centrality has another major role—it is able to identify *boundary spanners* —people that act as bridges between two or more communities that otherwise would not be able to communicate to each other. For example, yours truly considers himself a boundary spanner between the academic world of computer science, and the world of music. My bona fides are good in both communities—a Ph.D. in computer science, and a long career as an in-demand sideman for both jazz and rock gigs. Consequently, if my social network was analyzed by an outsider, he would discover that two nearly disjointed groups have very few connection points except for myself and a few others (in fact, I have played in a rock band that consisted only of computer science Ph.Ds, so the overlap is not as uncommon as one might imagine).

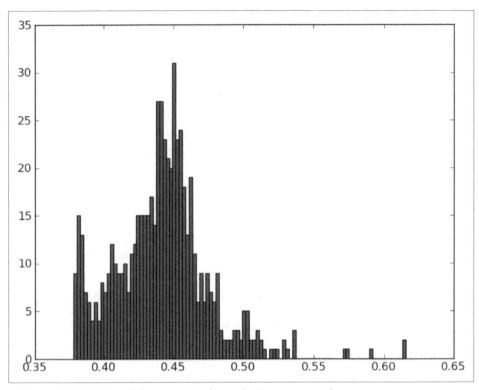

Figure 3-6. Distribution of closeness centrality in the Russian network

The way we measure betweenness is as follows; this algorithm is fairly time-consuming for large networks:

- Compute the shortest paths between every pair of nodes using Dijkstra's Algorithm.
- For every node I in the network:
    —Count the number of shortest paths that I is on
- Normalize the numbers to bring your results to the 0-1 range.

In the bow-tie network in Figure 3-7, all nodes' betweenness centrality is 0, except D, whose betweenness centrality is ~ 0.6:

```
>>> net.betweenness_centrality(bow)
{'A': 0.0, 'C': 0.0, 'B': 0.0, 'E': 0.0, 'D': 0.59999999999999998, 'G': 0.0, 'F': 0.0}
```

Let us now calculate betweenness for the Russian network. Computing it on all 81000 nodes is too time-consuming, so for the purpose of this exercise we will only compute it on the core network:

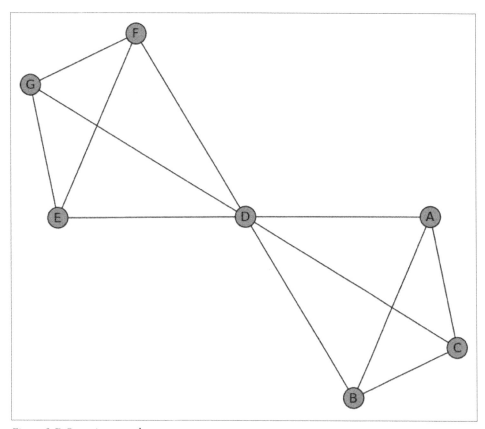

Figure 3-7. Bow-tie network

```
>>> b=net.betweenness_centrality(core10)
>>> bs=sorted_map(b)
>>> bs[:10]
[('valerois', 0.21148671833684918), ('azbukivedi', 0.090685469837536059),
('bagira', 0.06415743377135999), ('karial', 0.049436498735116997),
('kpoxa_e', 0.040441270584172219), ('snorapp', 0.026244420037490532),
('borisakunin', 0.023042685592280537), ('kirulya', 0.022601460496828561),
('eprst2000', 0.021420612080769161), ('doctor_liza', 0.020507259543668853)]
```

As you see, a pattern is emerging—familiar names will pop up in the top ten of the
three centrality metrics, possibly in different order. Every network has a certain "elite
group" of users that will be noticeable in the same way—often, two out of three, or all
three centrality metrics will land a person in the top ten. If the target use of the analysis
is for directed advertising, information operations, or intelligence collection (whether
for business or government), these elite groups form a perfect target.

Putting It Together

Since it is easy to measure basic centrality metrics for all nodes, we can now interpret what combinations of these metrics mean—and thus work on making some conclusions about the Russian bloggers and gossipers that we unwittingly recruited as our subjects.

Table 3-1. Combining centrality metrics

Metric	Low Degree	Low Closeness	Low Betweenness
High Degree		Ego is embedded in a cluster that is far from the rest of the network	Ego's connections are redundant—the world passes him by
High Closeness	Key player tied to important or active others		Ego is in a dense, active cluster at the center of events—with many others

```
## make a list of the elite group by merging top ten groups for 3 centrality metrics
names1=[x[0] for x in ds[:10]]
names2=[x[0] for x in cs[:10]]
names3=[x[0] for x in bs[:10]]

## use Python sets to compute a union of the sets
names=list(set(names1) | set(names2) | set (names3))

## build a table with centralities
table=[[name,d[name],c[name],b[name]] for name in names]
```

Table 3-2. The elite group in the Russian network

Name	Degree	Closeness	Betweenness
valerois	232	0.6137040715	0.211486718337
bagira	1481	0.589694656489	0.0641574337714
kpoxa_e	946	0.572222222222	0.0404412705842
tareeva	2970	0.475750577367	0.0058846904873
elladkin	2616	0.464661654135	0.0157282364002
azbukivedi	2541	0.615537848606	0.0906854698375
kirulya	2398	0.536458333333	0.0226014604968
karial	2717	0.573816155989	0.0494364987351
masha_koroleva	2683	0.495987158909	0.0126245435456
doctor_liza	3046	0.48168355417	0.0205072595437
borisakunin	4691	0.531841652324	0.0230426855923
samoleg	2597	0.475384615385	0.0156636804634
yelya	582	0.536924413553	0.0152393267528
zina_korzina	2596	0.492822966507	0.00896432034117

Name	Degree	Closeness	Betweenness
snorapp	2707	0.530017152659	0.0262444200375
eprst2000	2510	0.528656971771	0.0214206120808
cheger	2887	0.399224806202	0.000717430487753
angerona	752	0.535064935065	0.0192380064535

Table 3-2 shows the elite group of the Russian social network. Almost all of the members of this group have a high closeness centrality—but only *valerois* sticks out in terms of betweenness centrality.

Who Is a "Gray Cardinal?"

Don Corleone did not have many strong ties. He was a man of few words, yet he could make an offer you can't refuse. Don Corleone surrounded himself with his sons and his trusted *capos*, who in turn, handled the day to day management issues of the family.[7] If we used network metrics such as degree centrality, betweenness or closeness, Don Corleone would be largely invisible in the network—which is the point of how his organization was created.

Positions such as Don Corleone's can have an immense power; by knowing well-connected people, they can exploit this information and information asymmetry to further their own plans, while staying largely in the shadows.

An éminence grise (French for "gray cardinal") is a powerful advisor or decision-maker who operates secretly or unofficially. This phrase originally referred to François Leclerc du Tremblay, the righthand man of Cardinal Richelieu. Although he never achieved that rank, it is probable that those around him may have addressed him thus in reference to the considerable influence this "gray friar" held over "his Eminence the Cardinal." [8]

Since grey cardinals exist in social networks, there must be a metric to find them!

Philip Bonacich proposed that instead of simply adding the number of links to compute degree, one should weight each of the links by the degree of the node at the other end of the link (i.e., well-connected people are worth more than badly connected people).[9] He designed an algorithm to iteratively compute these weights, and thus to produce a centrality metric where grey cardinals can be detected.

---

7. I am totally not doing justice to the film or the novel, but I need an example. Please bear with me.

8. Source: Wikipedia (*http://en.wikipedia.org/wiki/Gray_cardinal*)

9. Bonacich, P. "Some unique properties of eigenvector centrality." *Social Networks* 29 (2007), 555-564.

Eigenvector centrality is like a recursive version of degree centrality. The algorithm works roughly as follows:

1. Start by assigning a centrality score of 1 to all nodes ($v\_i = 1$ for all i in the network).
2. Recompute the scores of each node as a weighted sum of centralities of all nodes in a node's neighborhood:

$$v_i = \sum_{j \in N} x_{i,j} * v_j$$

3. Normalize **v** by dividing each value by the largest value.
4. Repeat steps 2 and 3 until the values of **v** stop changing.

A node is central to the extent that the node is connected to others who are central. An actor who is high on eigenvector centrality is connected to many actors who are themselves connected to many actors.

In practice

NetworkX provides an implementation of eigenvector centrality:

```
>>> eigenvector_centrality(g)
```

Note that this is an iterative algorithm, where for each node one must iterate through its neighbors to compute the weighted degree. Thus, every iteration of the algorithm takes on the order of *O(nodes*average_degree)* operations, and there could be hundreds of iterations. Long story short: eigenvector centrality is not realistic to compute on very large networks.

In the Russian network, the top eigenvector centralities belong to:

'valerois'	0.250535826
'bagira'	0.222453253
'azbukivedi'	0.215904343
'kpoxa_e'	0.207785523
'boctok'	0.164058289
'yelya'	0.160704177
'mamaracha'	0.159064962
'karial'	0.15127215
'angerona'	0.146023845
'marinka'	0.127491521

Many of them (bostok, bagira, azbukivedi) also have high degree centralities. However, a few (mamaracha and valerois) have low degree, high betweenness, and high eigenvector centrality. This largely means that they are in a position we call a *Boundary Spanner* (more on these later), essentially standing between two dense and popular clusters, but not being a full-time member of any of them.

Klout Score

Klout Score is a metric computed upon all of your social media activity (Figure 3-8). Klout samples a variety of activities that a person can engage in—from Twitter posts and number of followers, to activity on Facebook and a number of other networks. Their data sources can be better than these available to the "mere mortals"; they have access to the full Twitter "firehose" feed, and their business model exchanges access to Klout scores for Klout's access to the user's personal data.

Klout applies a proprietary formula to weigh all of its users on a percentage scale, with celebrities like *@ladygaga* and *@justinbieber* topping the scale at 100%, a strong "middle class" inhabiting the 20%-50% range, and the majority of casual Twitter users located way below this mark.

Figure 3-8. Klout score anatomy

However, to an outsider, the Klout score is basically a degree centrality metric across a number of services and types of messages. As such, it does not capture the idea of boundary spanning, or the idea of dense clusters and communities separated by conversation topics (or, indeed, by language). *@ladygaga* may be influential in the pop-culture circles, but is she influential among French scientists? Unlikely.

Application of an undifferentiated centrality score across a very wide network is bound to bring a result that is difficult to interpret in a specific context—so what Klout gains in simplicity of presentation, it loses in ability to make fine-grained predictions.

PageRank—How Google Measures Centrality

PageRank[10] turns the idea of centrality on its head. Instead of centrality "radiating forward" from a node and being one of the node's properties, PageRank centrality is determined trough incoming links. PageRank was originally developed for indexing web pages, but can be applied to social networks as well, as long as they are directed graphs—for example, a retweet network on Twitter is an excellent candidate.

Simplified PageRank algorithm

PageRank is scaled between 0 and 1 and represents the likelihood that a person following links (i.e., traversing the network, "surfing" the web, etc) will arrive at a particular page or encounter a particular person. A 0.5 probability is commonly interpreted as a "50% chance" of an event. Hence, a PageRank of 0.5 means there is a 50% chance that a person clicking on a random link will be directed to the document with the 0.5 PageRank.

Let us step through a simplified version of PageRank (Figure 3-9):

1. Assume a small network of four nodes: (A)lice, (B)ob, (C)arol, and (D)avid.
2. Initially, assign equal probability to A,B,C, and D: $PR(A)=PR(B)=PC(C)=PR(D)=0.25$.
3. If B, C, and D only link to A, A's PageRank would be computed as $PR(A)=PR(B)+PR(C)+PR(D)=0.25+0.25+0.25=0.75$.
4. If a page has multiple outgoing links (*outdegree > 1*) then its PageRank contribution is equally divided by all of the link targets: $PRc(A) = PR(A)/out\text{-}degree(A)$.
5. Suppose that page B has a link to page C as well as to page A, while page D has links to all three pages. The value of the link-votes is divided among all the outbound links on a page. Thus, page B gives a vote worth 0.125 to page A and a vote worth 0.125 to page C. Only one third of D's PageRank is counted for A's PageRank (approximately 0.083).

---

10. The name "PageRank" is a trademark of Google, and the PageRank process has been patented (U.S. Patent 6,285,999). However, the patent is assigned to Stanford University and not to Google. Google has exclusive license rights on the patent from Stanford University.

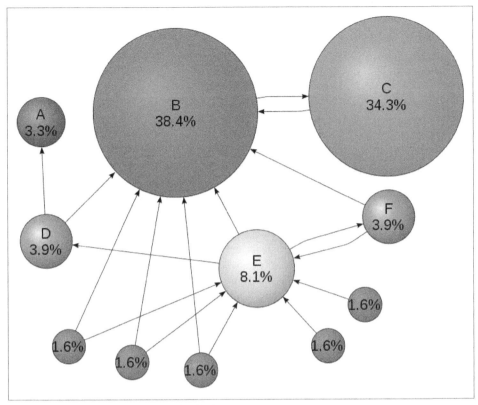

Figure 3-9. Example of the page rank calculation

6. In the general case, PageRank can be computed as $PR(N)=Sum\_\{i \in nodes\} (PR(i)/ out\_degree(i))$.

7. Repeat calculation of PageRank for all nodes until the values stabilize.

PageRank is an iterative process, otherwise known as an *anytime algorithm*. That is, at any given time it will return a result, but if more time is given to it, the quality of results improves greatly. When first started, it will give a highly inaccurate result; this result will quickly improve with iterations until it reaches a point of stability (*convergence*) or until the user runs out of time and patience. In a way, PageRank is similar to eigenvector centrality—but the algorithm scales much better to very large networks and networks that change over time.

In the Google implementation (and, indeed, in most other implementations), there is a damping parameter that reduces the potential oscillation of the system, which could cause the entire operation not to converge. There is a well-documented procedure for computing this parameter statistically, but, as a rule of thumb, the default damping factor of 0.85 works well.

NetworkX contains a useful implementation of PageRank:

```
>>> pr=net.pagerank(g)
```

Running the algorithm for the same Russian LiveJournal data as before, we get a fairly similar result for the top 10 members:

```
[('valerois', 0.25053582622281872),
 ('bagira', 0.22245325327537924),
 ('azbukivedi', 0.21590434284063595),
 ('kpoxa_e', 0.20778552299062297),
 ('boctok', 0.16405828921767182),
 ('yelya', 0.16070417738193199),
 ('mamaracha', 0.15906496179945631),
 ('karial', 0.15127214975509715),
 ('angerona', 0.14602384461951823),
 ('marinka', 0.12749152062345798), ...
```

The main difference lies in the fact that PageRank represents a "flow of trust" or "flow of influence" rather than a more abstract graph-theoretic concept like betweenness. While PageRank computation is local in nature (only immediate neighbors are taken into consideration), its iterative nature allows global influence to propagate through the network—although much attenuated, just like in the real world.[11]

What Can't Centrality Metrics Tell Us?

Centrality metrics, while representing a first valiant approach at understanding the social network forces, are essentially point-measures on the network. What these metrics do not tell us is how (or, indeed, why) the high-centrality visionary (or a loudmouth) is surrounded by a gaggle of acolytes, what forces make people choose sides in a debate, and what forces bring networks together and tear them apart. For that, we have to look deeper than point-measures. In the next chapter, we'll explore triads—arguably, the smallest group of people that one could possibly call "a society." From these triads we'll develop larger cliques and clusters, learn how to find them in real data, and where this could lead us.

---

11. The spread and attenuation of influence over network links is discussed at length in Chapter 6.

## CHAPTER 4

Cliques, Clusters and Components

In the previous chapter, we mainly talked about properties of individuals in a social network. In this chapter, we start working with progressively larger chunks of the network, analyzing not just the individuals and their connection patterns, but entire subgraphs and clusters. We'll explore what it means to be in a triad and what benefits and stresses can come from being in a structural hole.

First, we will deconstruct the network by progressively removing parts to find its core(s); then, we'll re-construct the network from its constituent parts—diads, triads, cliques, clans and clusters.

Components and Subgraphs

To start teasing apart the networks into analyzable parts, let us first make a couple definitions:

- A *subgraph* is a subset of the nodes of a network, and all of the edges linking these nodes. Any group of nodes can form a subgraph—and further down we will describe several interesting ways to use this.

- Component subgraphs (or simply *components*) are portions of the network that are disconnected from each other. Before the meeting of Romeo and Juliet, the two families were quite separate (save for the conflict ties), and thus could be treated as components.

Many real networks (especially these collected with random sampling) have multiple components. One could argue that this is a sampling error (which is very possible) — but at the same time, it may just mean that the ties between components are outside of the scope of the sampling and may in fact be irrelevant.

Analyzing Components with Python

The Egypt uprising retweet network is a good example of a network with many components. The datafile included with this book was collected through a 1% Twitter feed and is largely incomplete. Let us load the data and examine it. NetworkX has a function for isolating connected components (*connected_component_subgraphs(e)*); the function returns an array of Graph objects corresponding to each of the connected components:

```
>>> e=net.read_pajek("egypt_retweets.net")
>>> len(e)
25178
>>> len(net.connected_component_subgraphs(e))
3122
```

What this means is that the retweet network contains ~25,000 nodes, but the network is split into over 3,000 component subgraphs. Let us now study how these component sizes are distributed:

```
>>> import matplotlib.pyplot as plot
>>> x=[len(c) for c in net.connected_component_subgraphs(e)]
>>> plot.hist()
```

Of 3,100 components, 2,471 are of size 1—these are called "isolates" and should be removed from the network. There are 546 components of size 2 (i.e., a single retweet), 67 of size 3, 14 of size 4, and 11 of size 5. By the time we reach component size 10 or greater, the numbers are very small:

```
>>> [len(c) for c in net.connected_component_subgraphs(e) if len(c) > 10]
[17762, 64, 16, 16, 14, 13, 11, 11]
```

What this means is that there is one giant component of size ~17,000, 7 components of size < 100, and nothing in between.

In this particular case, we can treat the giant component as the whole network; however it is still too large to make interesting inferences.

Islands in the Net

One technique for analyzing networks is called "the island method" (see Figure 4-1); it is particularly well-suited to valued networks such as the Egypt Twitter network that we are using as sample data.

The island method works as follows: imagine our network as an island with a complex terrain, where the height of each point on the terrain is defined by the value of a node (e.g., degree centrality) or edge (e.g., number of retweets). Now let us imagine that the water level around this island is rising slowly, leaving portions of the landscape underwater. When the valleys in the island are flooded, the island essentially splits into smaller islands—revealing where the highest peaks are, and making these peaks

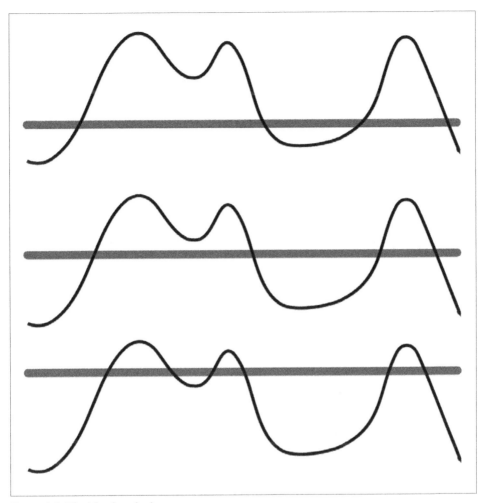

Figure 4-1. The island method

smaller. It is possible to raise the water level so high that the entire island will disappear, so this method needs to be applied judiciously to reveal meaningful results.

In terms of networks, this means that the giant component gets split up into smaller components, and areas with the strongest amount of retweeting activity (subcores) become their own components that can be analyzed separately.

The first thing we need to implement for the *island method* is a function to virtually raise the water level. The function below takes a graph, and applies a threshold ("water level"), letting all edges above a certain value through, and removing all others. Don't worry—it returns a copy of the original graph, so it's non-destructive:

```
def trim_edges(g, weight=1):
    g2=net.Graph()
    for f, to, edata in g.edges(data=True):
        if edata['weight'] > weight:
            g2.add_edge(f,to,edata)
    return g2
```

Now, let's define how the water level should be raised. We will compute evenly spaced thresholds and produce a list of networks at each water level:

```
def island_method(g, iterations=5):
    weights= [edata['weight'] for f,to,edata in g.edges(data=True)]

    mn=int(min(weights))
    mx=int(max(weights))
    #compute the size of the step, so we get a reasonable step in iterations
    step=int((mx-mn)/iterations)

    return [[threshold, trim_edges(g, threshold)] for threshold in range(mn,mx,step)]
```

This function will return a list of graph objects, each corresponding to a specific water level.

Now let's isolate the biggest component of the Egypt Retweet Network, and separate it into subparts using the island method:

```
>>> cc=net.connected_component_subgraphs(e)[0]
>>> islands=island_method(cc)
>>> for i in islands:
...    # print the threshold level, size of the graph, and number of connected components
...    print i[0], len(i[1]), len(net.connected_component_subgraphs(i[1]))

    1 12360 314
    62  27 11
    123  8 3
    184  5 2
    245  5 2
```

What does this mean? When all links with a value of 1 (i.e., single retweets) are dropped, the network separates into 314 island subgraphs—each representing a group of people retweeting repeatedly from each other. Since single retweets could be considered accidental, this is a very useful result—repeated retweets are more likely to happen between groups of people that communicate repeatedly and thus have developed some kind of a trust relationship.

Thresholding at the value of 62 (i.e., 62 repeat retweets for each pair of nodes) reveals that there are only 27 nodes left, in 11 islands. In this case, it's the highest meaningful threshold—the remaining 27 nodes are the people most actively involved in the Tahrir Square protests, and journalists covering the events.

It may take some trial and error, but a well-tuned "water level" can yield a very meaningful analysis of a large network—instantly zeroing in on the cores of the most activity.

Subgraphs—Ego Networks

Ego networks are subnetworks that are centered on a certain node. On Facebook and LinkedIn, these are simply described as "your network"—but you can only access your own ego networks, and can't do a broader survey. Having a larger dataset allows us to survey and compare ego networks of various people.

We derive ego networks by running a breath-first search (described in "Breadth-First Traversal" on page 30), and limiting the depth of our search (network radius) to a small value, usually not more than 3. While in traditional BFS we build a tree of links we followed to get to a node, to produce an ego network we capture *all* links between node's neighbors.

To explain the reasoning behind using a small search depth, we should revisit the idea of what it means to be connected in a social network, and what network distance means. In the most basic case, a link means that "Alice is friends with Bob," a distance of 2 means "Carol is a friend of a friend of Alice," and a distance of 3 means that "Dave is a friend of a friend of a friend of Alice." Intuitively, we understand that while we know quite a bit about our friends, and we know something about some of our friends' friends, we know nearly nothing about our friends' friends' friends.

Formally, this concept is known as a *Horizon of Observability*,[1] a concept loosely borrowed from physics and the notion of the observable universe. Noah Friedkin observed that in social networks, people had a relatively high degree of knowledge of their own immediate social networks (~30% error rate), which is about as good as self-reported data can be. The error rate jumps to 70% for 2 degrees of separation, and to nearly 100% at 3.

In online networks such as Twitter, with a significantly looser definition of a "friend" and computer-facilitated retention of information, the useful radius of the ego network is much larger. However, trust and influence still travel over the less-reliable "wetware" interpersonal channels, so it would be a mistake to consider ego networks with a radius over 3. Depth-first search may be used instead to determine the penetration of a message via a sequence of retweets—a technique that we will address in Chapter 6.

Extracting and Visualizing Ego Networks with Python

Extraction of ego networks is quite simple—as NetworkX provides a ready-made function to do the job:

```
>>> net.ego_graph(cc,'justinbieber')
<networkx.classes.multigraph.MultiGraph object at 0x1ad54090>
```

---

1. Friedkin, Noah. "Horizons of Observability and Limits of Informal Control in Organizations." *Social Forces* 1983.

Yes, believe it or not, Justin Bieber is in the Egypt Retweet dataset. His ego network was shown early on in the book, in Figure 1-11.

The ego_graph function returns a NetworkX graph object, and all the usual metrics (degree, betweenness, etc.,) can be computed on it.

However, a couple other simple metrics stand out as well. Knowing the size of an ego network is important to understand the reach of the information that a person can transmit (or, conversely, have access to).

The other metric is called *clustering coefficient*—essentially, it measures the proportion of your friends that are also friends with each other (i.e., what amount of mutual trust people have for each other). This metric can be applied to entire networks—but in a large network with widely varying densities and multiple cores, average clustering is difficult to interpret. In ego networks, the interpretation is simple—dense ego networks with a lot of mutual trust have a high clustering coefficient. Star networks with a single broadcast node and passive listeners have a low clustering coefficient.

Let us explore a couple ego networks in the Egypt data:

```
## we need to convert the ego network from a Multi-graph to a simple Graph
>>> bieb = net.Graph(net.ego_graph(cc,'justinbieber', radius=2))
>>> len(bieb)
22
>>> net.average_clustering(bieb)
0.0
```

The celebrity status of Justin Bieber doesn't help him in this particular case—of his (at the time) 9 million followers, only 22 have retweeted his messages about the Egyptian uprising. His clustering coefficient shows that he is a pure broadcaster and is not embedded in a trust network of fans—or, at least, he is not in a trust network that cares about world politics.[2]

Let us now explore a celebrity of a different kind—Wael Ghonim, the face of the new generation of Egyptians, a Google executive, and a prolific tweeter:

```
>>> ghonim= net.Graph(net.ego_graph(cc,'Ghonim', radius=2))
>>> len(ghonim)
3450
>>> net.average_clustering(ghonim)
0.22613518489812276
```

Not only does Wael Ghonim have a vastly larger retweet network (despite having 100 times fewer followers than Bieber), his ego network is a network of trust where people retweet messages from him and from each other—a network where a revolutionary message can easily spread and be sustained.

The structural hole and triadic analysis that we will discuss in the next section is also very applicable to ego networks—so stay tuned and improvise with your data!

---

2. This is a sad commentary upon American youth.

Triads

A triad is simply three nodes interlinked in some way. However, in triad analysis, things are really not so simple. All possible *undirected* triads are shown in Figure 4-2; as you can see, only the first two have all of their nodes interconnected, and thus present a significant interest. There are 16 possible *directed* triads, but we shall defer that discussion until a little later in the chapter.

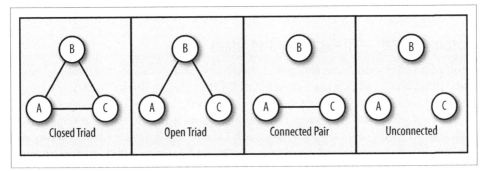

Figure 4-2. Triad shapes

The closed triad (on the left in Figure 4-2) represents a fully connected group: *A*, *B*, and *C* are connected to each other with equivalently strong ties. The most basic example of a triad like this is a "nuclear family"—mother (Alice), father (Bob) and a child (Carol). Of course, these triads can overlap—for example, the same mother and father might have another child (Dan), in which case there is not one triad, but 4:

```
[alice, bob, carol]
[alice, bob, dave]
[carol, dave, alice]
[carol, dave, bob]
```

This network structure represents perhaps the oldest piece of research in the entire field. In 1908, Georg Simmel, a contemporary of Max Weber and a member of his intellectual circles, authored a piece called "The Treatise on the Triad".[3]

He wrote that in a *dyad* (i.e., two nodes connected to each other), each person is able to retain their individuality while maintaining a close relationship. Exchange of information and ideas happens, but at the same time it does not subjugate the individual to the group. In a *triad*, the third individual becomes at a source of balance (providing second opinions and calming nerves). However, the third node is also a feedback loop —information from *A* can pass to *B*, then to *C*, and back to *A*—in a much distorted form, as a childrens' game of "Telephone" shows.

---

3. A modern translation and commentary can be found in:

   Nooteboom, Bart. "Simmel's Treatise on the Triad (1908)". *Journal of Institutional Economics* 2(2006) 365-383.

As a result of accumulating distortions, a triad over time generates a set of artifacts that are private to the triad—local jargon or nicknames, local norms and rules of behavior, shared stories. In a macro-context, sociologists would call an accumulation of these artifacts, *culture*.

Perhaps in a context of one triad, this is a very big word to use—but think of your own family or the families of your friends. Or, download an episode of ABC's "Wife Swap" reality show (mercifully cancelled in 2009) and watch cultures of two families collide on reality TV.[4]

Fraternity Study—Tie Stability and Triads

Another study in the same milieu was done by Newcomb. [5] In fact, this study is somewhat (disturbingly) similar to modern reality TV, but was conducted in the early 1960s. Imagine a fraternity in Michigan (yes, there was beer). At the beginning of a semester, 17 students (all white men) were recruited to live in a frat house for a semester, in exchange for their personal data. Every week, researchers interviewed every one of the students asking them to rank their interactions with their fraternity brothers from 1 (best) to 16 (worst).

The findings of this study were that:

- Asymmetric ties (e.g., "I like you more than you like me") were the least stable of all, lasting no more than two weeks.

- Symmetric ties (dyads where 2 people like each other about equally) were significantly more stable.

- Triadic structures were the most stable over time, with students smoothing over conflicts, organizing events (parties?) together, and overall defining the tone of interaction among the fraternity brothers.

Triads and Terrorists

In the beginning of the book ("Informal Networks in Terrorist Cells" on page 11), we mentioned that Al Qaeda cells were often sequestered in safe-houses during training and preparation for terrorist attacks. This sequestration forced the cells to form a dense triadic structure, with everyone embedded in triads with everyone else. Combined with a virtual sensory deprivation (all information from the outside world arrived highly filtered through the cell leader), the groups generate their own cultural artifacts that go beyond nicknames and shared stories—but rather continue to define their identity as religious extremist and reinforcing their resolve to complete the attack.

---

4. The authors are not responsible for ensuing brain damage.

5. Newcomb T. *The acquaintance process*. New York: Holt, Reinhard & Winston, 1961.

The Hamburg Cell (which started the planning for 9/11 and ultimately participated in the attack) was—to quote Mark Sageman,[6] "just a bunch of guys." After studying the lives of 172 terrorists, Sageman found the most common factor driving them was the social ties within their cell. Most started as friends, colleagues, or relatives—and were drawn closer by bonds of friendship, loyalty, solidarity and trust, and rewarded by a powerful sense of belonging and collective identity.

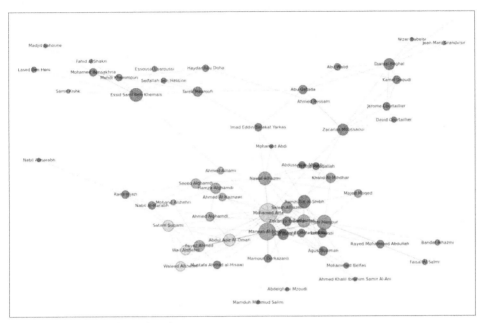

Figure 4-3. Network of 9/11 hijackers

In the book's GitHub repository (*https://github.com/maksim2042/SNABook/chapter4*), you can find the data used to generate the picture in Figure 4-3 [7] and analyze it yourself. The data is supplied in an edge-list file, in a format resembling the following:

```
Hani Hanjour,Majed Moqed,5,1
Hani Hanjour,Nawaf Alhazmi,5,1
Hani Hanjour,Khalid Al-Mihdhar,5,1
```

6. Sageman, Marc. *Understanding Terror Networks*. University of Pennsylvania Press, 2004.

7. The original dataset was provided by Valdis Krebs.

The first column is the name of the "from" node, the second column is the name of the "to" node, and the following two numbers signify the strength of tie (5=strong tie, 1=weak tie); and the level to which the tie has been verified (1 = confirmed close contact, 2 = various recorded interactions, 3 = potential or planned or unconfirmed interactions).

To read this file, we will not be able to use NetworkX's built-in file readers, but we can build one in just a few lines of code:

```
import csv ## we'll use the built-in CSV library
import networkx as net

# open the file
in_file=csv.reader(open('9_11_edgelist.txt','rb'))

g=net.Graph()
for line in in_file:
    g.add_edge(line[0],line[1],weight=line[2],conf=line[3])
```

We also have an attribute file that marks the 19 hijackers by the flight that they were on. Let's read this file as well:

```
#first, let's make sure that all nodes in the graph have the 'flight' attribute
for n in g.nodes_iter(): g.node[n]['flight']='None'

attrb=csv.reader(open('9_11_attrib.txt','rb'))
for line in attrb:
    g.node[line[0]]['flight']=line[1]
```

 There are two ways to list nodes in the graph. g.nodes() produces a list of nodes, and g.nodes_iter() produces a Python *iterator*. An iterator is limited to use in loops only—but takes significantly less memory and is faster on large graphs.

If you plotted the network right now using the default net.draw(g) function, you would find that the network consists of several disconnected components. This is due to the data being largely fragmentary and incomplete; we should concern ourselves with the largest component of the network only:

```
# Connected_component_subgraphs() returns a list of components,
# sorted largest to smallest
components=net.connected_component_subgraphs(g)

# pick the first and largest component
cc = components[0]
```

We use a custom plotting function in *multimode.py* to plot the picture. The function reads node attributes and assigns colors to them based on attribute values, creating a custom color-map on the fly:

```
import networkx as net
import matplotlib.pyplot as plot
from collections import defaultdict

def plot_multimode(m,layout=net.spring_layout,
type_string='type',filename_prefix='',output_type='pdf'):

    ## create a default color order and an empty color-map
    colors=['r','g','b','c','m','y','k']
    colormap={}
    d=net.degree(m)   #we use degree for sizing nodes
    pos=layout(m)   #compute layout

    #Now we need to find groups of nodes that need to be colored differently
    nodesets=defaultdict(list)
    for n in m.nodes():
        t=m.node[n][type_string]
        nodesets[t].append(n)

    ## Draw each group of nodes separately, using its own color settings
    print "drawing nodes..."
    i=0
    for key in nodesets.keys():
        ns=[d[n]*100 for n in nodesets[key]]
        net.draw_networkx_nodes(m,pos,nodelist=nodesets[key], node_size=ns,
                                node_color=colors[i], alpha=0.6)
        colormap[key]=colors[i]
        i+=1
        if i==len(colors):
            i=0   ### wrap around the colormap if we run out of colors
    print colormap

    ## Draw edges using a default drawing mechanism
    print "drawing edges..."
    net.draw_networkx_edges(m,pos,width=0.5,alpha=0.5)
    net.draw_networkx_labels(m,pos,font_size=8)
    plot.axis('off')
    if filename_prefix is not '':
        plot.savefig(filename_prefix+'.'+output_type)
```

Finally, we plot the networks:

```
import multimode as mm

# type-string tells the function what attribute to differentiate on
mm.plot_multimode(cc,type_string='flight')
```

Once we establish the tools for triadic analysis, you can use this data as a test-bed to understand the way triads work, and also potentially link up to the rich literature on terrorism studies.

The "Forbidden Triad" and Structural Holes

My friend *Bob*[8] has a problem. You see, he is in love with two women. One is a spirited beauty from Eastern Europe (let's call her *Alice*), and the other a happy-go-lucky girl from South America named *Carolina*. Either of the two would have made an excellent match for Bob, but yet he can't decide. When Bob is with Alice, he longs for Carolina and her lighthearted attitude, and when he's with Carolina he longs for Alice and her beauty and deep conversations. As a result, after all these years, Bob is still pathologically single.

In terms of networks, Bob's predicament looks like the second triad in Figure 4-2. *B* is linked to *A*, and to *C*—but *A* is not in any way linked to *C*, and should stay that way if Bob wants to keep up the ruse. Every day, this is adding more and more stress to Bob's life as he needs to coordinate his schedule to make sure *A* and *C* never meet, but also needs to make sure that he doesn't "spill the beans" by failing to remember what he told *A* or *C*—or by accidentally passing information from *A* to *C*. As a result, *Bob* is ridden with angst, and the whole thing is really not working out in his favor.

My other friend, a *Banker*, has a very similar situation in terms of network connections, but in fact is rather happy about it. His *A* stands for *AmeriCorp, Inc* and *C* for *CorpAmerica, Inc. AmeriCorp, Inc.* deposits money in his bank, expecting an interest payments of 5%. *CorpAmerica, Inc.* takes out loans, paying an interest rate of 7%. *B* gets to keep the spread in interest rates—the 2% difference between what *C* pays and what *A* expects in interest. In case of my friend, this 2% spread is big enough to pay for a large house, a late-model BMW, an elite country-club membership, and many other material possessions that he enjoys rather conspicuously. Had *A* and *C* ever got together for a friendly game of golf, they could agree on *A* loaning money to *C* directly at a rate of 6% and realize that both could benefit by cutting out the middleman. *Banker B* would be rather upset if that happens.

Despite completely different stories behind the triads, *Bob's* and *Banker's* interests are exactly the same. They need to make sure that the two ends of their open-triad network never communicate directly—that is, never form a link.

The name for this triad varies depending on who you ask. Some researchers call it "the forbidden triad"—because, like Bob, they think it is related to stress, anxiety, and questionable morals of dating two women at the same time. Others call it a "structural hole" or a "brokerage structure" and relate number of structural holes to a person's ability to perform as an entrepreneur, a banker, a broker or a real-estate agent.

---

8. Names have been changed to protect the guilty, but the stories are real, if somewhat stylized.

Ron Burt[9] showed in his studies that businessmen who maintained many structural holes had a significantly higher rate of success in a competitive marketplace. This was predicated on two things—the success of businessmen was based on their ability to exploit and trade on asymmetric information, and the businessmen had to have a high tolerance for stress involved in creating and maintaining "arbitrage opportunities."

Structural Holes and Boundary Spanning

Structural holes have another important mission—since they can span asymmetric information (as both of my friends exploit), they can also bridge entire communities. Both authors of this book are professionals in the field of social network analysis (Max teaches it, and Alex writes analytic software), and professional musicians. In fact, we met at a rock festival where our respective bands performed.

So—a triad that includes Max, Max's closest collaborator in science, and the drummer in his band is indeed a structural hole. The scientist and the drummer would share some basic understanding of English, but would hardly find enough topics for conversation; a social network tie between them is nearly impossible due to the *social distance* (a term we will explore further when we discuss information diffusion in Chapter 6).

Our communities (scientists and musicians) intersect more often than one would imagine; Max used to perform with a band that consisted entirely of professors, and a rock band consisting entirely of neuroscientists (called The Amygdaloids) [10] has actually been signed by a label.

However, these boundary spanners (scientist musicians and musician scientists) are still relatively rare compared to the number of people that are only professional musicians or scientists. As a result, the intersection between two communities looks somewhat like Figure 4-4.

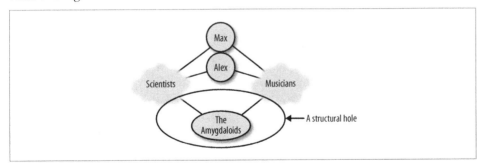

Figure 4-4. Clouds and boundary spanners

9. Burt, Ronald. *Structural Holes: The Structure of Competition*. Cambridge, MA: Harvard University Press, 1992.

10. www.amygdaloids.com

In fact, this sort of thing happens on many levels. If we drilled into the "Scientists" cloud, we would find that it consists of major fields (biology, computer science, humanities, etc), and if we drill down further we find that fields consist of subfields, all linked by structural holes.

In the scientific community, this is especially important since many new discoveries are interdisciplinary in nature. For example, James Fowler[11] works at the intersection of social network analysis and neuroscience.

Some other fields (economics is one) discourage communication and cross-publication between subfields, and are very protective of their theories. In these cases, a structural hole position between, say, Austrian and neo-classical economics would be very stressful to sustain—more like *Bob*'s predicament than that of the *Banker*.

Triads in Politics

Figure 4-5 shows a network of political cooperation among the countries in the Caucasus. [12] The Caucasus is a very interesting place in terms of modern geopolitics (see the map in Figure 4-6). It's a fairly small patch of uniquely beautiful mountainous landscape that is sandwiched between Russia on the north, and Turkey and Iran to the south. Its population is a tumultuous mix of Christian and Muslim nations, and their shifting allegiances to the West, Russia, or Turkey have (starting with the disintegration of Soviet Union) created a geopolitical landscape that is full of surprises (mostly unpleasant ones, at least for the local population).

The network in the figure is built by looking at the joint political statements and agreements made by the countries and republics of the Caucasus, Russia, Turkey, EU, and the United States, and clearly shows the different governing styles of Russia and the West. The Russia-centric side of the network shows a system rich in structural holes. Russia is truly in charge, and lateral ties between peripheral actors are almost non-existent.

The single lateral tie is between South Ossetia and Abkhazia. At the time of this study, both of these areas were still technically a part of Georgia—but the fact that they had no allegiance to Georgia was quite apparent at the time. Within two years, South Ossetia became the site of a short but bloody attempt by the Georgian army to squash the separatist movement (alternatively, this was a Russian provocation to cement its influence in the region, depending on whether one listens to Russian or American news sources). Shortly thereafter, both South Ossetia and Abkhazia declared their independence and allied themselves formally with Russia.

11. At the University of California, San Diego (*http://jhfowler.ucsd.edu/*)

12. This data comes from a project I did in 2006 in collaboration with the Southern Federal University of Russia.

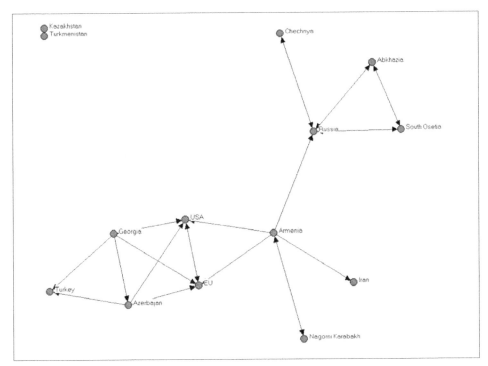

Figure 4-5. Political cooperation in the Caucasus

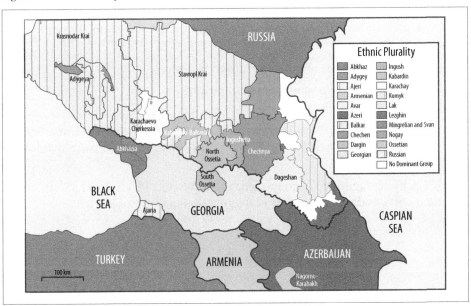

Figure 4-6. The Caucasus—an ethnic and linguistic melting pot

Meanwhile, the Western end of the network shows a pattern of closure and multilateral ties. This may be less conducive to influence from the superpowers, as lateral ties reduce efficiency of direct influence. However, at the same time the triadic structures are more stable and require less force to maintain.

Directed Triads

But enough theory, let's write some code!

Figure 4-7 shows all possible directed triads. In a directed triad, we consider edges that are both one-way and bidirectional; thus instead of 4 possible triads we have 16 variations. We will turn to interpretation of these shapes in a bit, but first let us define a way to catalogue them. This method of counting and cataloguing triads is somewhat arcane, but is a standard for the academic literature in the field and dates back to 1972.[13]

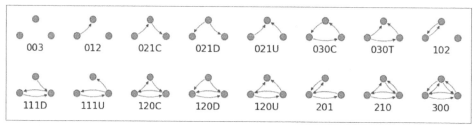

Figure 4-7. Triad census in directed networks

The triads are numbered 1-16, and have a code associated with them. The code reads like this:

- The first number is the number of bidirectional edges.
- The second number is the number of single edges.
- The third number is the number of "non-existent" edges.
- A letter code to distinguish directed variations of the same triad—U for "up," D for "down," C for "circle," and T for "transitive" (i.e., having 2 paths that lead to the same endpoint).

Triads 1-3 in the figure are unconnected, triads 4-8 and 11 represent variations on structural holes, and triads 9,10 and 12-16 are variations on closed triads.

13. Davis, J.A. and S. Leinhardt. "The Structure of Positive Interpersonal Relations in Small Groups." In *Sociological Theories in Progress*, volume 2, ed. J. Berger. Boston: Houghton Mifflin, 1972.

Analyzing Triads in Real Networks

The process of triadic analysis in a real network is called the *triad census*. In this process, for every node we count occurrences of the 16 types of triads to determine the node's role in the network structure. For example, a node with many occurrences of triads 4, 7, and 11 (i.e., rich in outgoing links and structural holes) is a *source* of information or possibly a group leader.

To run the triad census, we will need an algorithm that is not included in the NetworkX —the triadic census algorithm.[14] Download the Chapter4 package from GitHub,[15] change the directory to the location of downloaded files, and start Python:

```
>>> import networkx as net
>>> import tradic
>>> import draw_triads
```

The `draw_triads` command will reproduce Figure 4-7.

Now, let us apply the triadic census to some sample data (specifically to the kite network in Figure 4-8):

```
## generate a directed version of the classic "Kite Graph"
>>> g=net.DiGraph(net.krackhardt_kite_graph())

## Run the triadic census
>>> census, node_census = triadic.triadic_census(g)
>>> census
{'201': 24, '021C': 0, '021D': 0, '210': 0,
'120U': 0, '030C': 0, '003': 22, '300': 11,
'012': 0, '021U': 0, '120D': 0, '102': 63,
'111U': 0, '030T': 0, '120C': 0, '111D': 0}
```

The triadic census function returns two results—a Python *dict* with overall results for the network, and a *dict-of-dicts* containing the same results for individual nodes.

In the kite graph, the procedure has counted 24 structural-hole triads (code 201), and 11 closed triads (code 300). What this means is that there are areas of high closure within the network, and areas with many structural holes. Which, of course, is apparent from the sample picture—but may not be so apparent for larger networks.

The ratio between structural hole and closed triads is also important—a hierarchy is largely composed of structural holes, while more egalitarian structures would have a higher ratio of closed triads.

14. This algorithm was written by Alex Levenson and Diederik van Liere and submitted to the NetworkX source tree; it may be included in the next release.

15. *https://github.com/maksim2042/SNABook/chapter4*

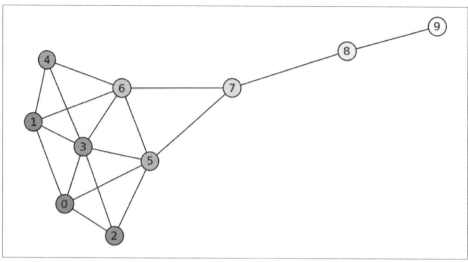

Figure 4-8. Krackhardt kite social network

In short, a triadic census lets one make high-level conclusions about the network structure in a macro form. However, the micro form is more interesting. The code below generates a triadic census table, and its results are in Table 4-1:

```
keys=node_census.values()[1].keys()

## Generate a table header
print '| Node |', ' | '.join(keys)

## Generate table contents
## A little magic is required to convert ints to strings
for k in node_census.keys():
    print '|', k, '|',' | '.join([str(v) for v in node_census[k].values()])
```

Table 4-1. Triad census in the kite network

Node	201	021C	021D	210	120U	030C	003	300	012	021U	120D	102	111U	030T	120C	111D
0	8	0	0	0	0	0	0	4	0	0	0	14	0	0	0	0
1	4	0	0	0	0	0	0	3	0	0	0	11	0	0	0	0
2	4	0	0	0	0	0	0	1	0	0	0	7	0	0	0	0
3	3	0	0	0	0	0	0	2	0	0	0	7	0	0	0	0
4	2	0	0	0	0	0	0	0	0	0	0	4	0	0	0	0
5	1	0	0	0	0	0	0	1	0	0	0	5	0	0	0	0
6	1	0	0	0	0	0	0	0	0	0	0	3	0	0	0	0
7	1	0	0	0	0	0	0	0	0	0	0	5	0	0	0	0
8	0	0	0	0	0	0	0	0	0	0	0	7	0	0	0	0
9	0	0	0	0	0	0	0	0	0	0	0	0	0	0	0	0

Let's look at the main types of triads: the closed triad (code 300) and the structural hole triad (code 201).

Real Data

Let's now run a triadic census on the 9/11 hijackers data we used earlier in the chapter, and find out who had the most cliques (closed triads, or triad *300*):

```
census, node_census = triadic.triadic_census(cc)
```

```
## get only the number of closed triads, and sort the list by the value, descending
closed_triads=[[-k,v] for k,v in sorted([[-node_census[k]['300'],k] for k in
node_census.keys()])]
```

The top person in the list has a familiar name: Mohammed Atta was part of the original Hamburg cell that planned the September 11th attacks, and served as the hijacker-pilot of American Airlines Flight 11, crashing the plane into the North Tower of the World Trade Center.

Cliques

While we might have an intuitive understanding of a clique in a social network as a cohesive group of people that are tightly connected to each other (and not tightly connected to people outside the group), in the field of SNA there is a formal mathematical definition that is quite a bit more rigorous.

A clique is defined as a *maximal complete subgraph* of a given graph—i.e., a group of people where everybody is connected directly to everyone else. The word "maximal" means that no other nodes can be added to the clique without making it less connected. Essentially, a clique consists of several overlapping closed triads, and inherits many of the culture-generating, and amplification properties of closed triads.

A clique must generate consensus or fall apart—which is why in the vernacular, cliques are often viewed in conflict with other cliques. It is, in fact, very easy to agree about conflict, and having a common enemy (or a group of common enemies) helps cliques unite. We will discuss some of the implication of conflict and cliques in Chapter 6.

But for now, let us see if we can locate cliques in some sample networks.

Detecting Cliques

As a test dataset, let us take another look at the data on geopolitics of the Caucasus. This time, we'll explore economic relations between the countries (Figure 4-9). The dataset rates level of economic cooperation on the scale of 0 to 1—where 1 is a close or exclusive tie, and 0 is the complete lack of economic cooperation:

```
>>> eco=net.read_pajek("economic.net")
>>> net.draw(eco)
```

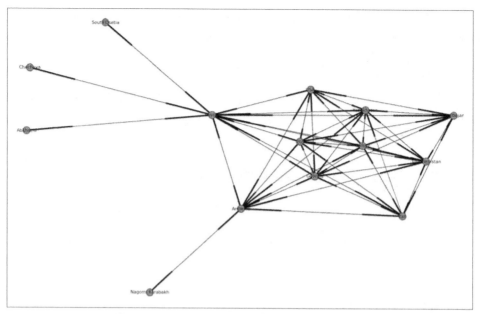

Figure 4-9. Economic alliances and joint activities in the Caucasus

The dataset clearly shows that there are two distinct sides to the region—the Western-centric side and the Russia-centric side; local and regional economic ties are frequently non-existent, as the nearest geographical neighbors (e.g., Armenia and Azerbaijan) consider each other to be enemies and structure their relationships with the super-powers accordingly. Iran and Turkey act as "spoilers"—a country with significant economic ties to Iran cannot have ties to the US, and thus is forced to ally itself with Russia. Of course, oil and natural gas interests play a significant role as well.

A structure like this is ripe for development of cliques. Let's see if we can find them. First, we will drop the low-level connections (< 0.5) to isolate the core:

```
>>> e2=trim_edges(eco, weight=0.5)
>>> cliques = list(net.find_cliques(eco))
>>> cliques
[['EU', 'Turkey', 'Russia'],
['EU', 'Turkey', 'USA'],
['EU', 'Azerbajan'],
['EU', 'Georgia'],
['EU', 'Kazakhstan', 'Russia'],
['EU', 'Kazakhstan', 'USA'], ['EU', 'Armenia'],
['South Osetia', 'Russia'],
['Nagorni Karabakh', 'Armenia'],
['Chechnya', 'Russia'],
['Abkhazia', 'Russia']]
```

Let's walk through the clique output. First,

[EU, Turkey, Russia], [EU, Turkey, USA]
> Represents the superpowers and the two sides of the debate whether Turkey should enter the EU as a member.

EU, Azerbaijan], [EU, Georgia]
> The Western-allied countries in the Caucasus; Azerbaijan is a major oil producer and a BP-owned pipeline crosses from Azerbaijan through Georgia on its way to the Black Sea.

[South Ossetia, Russia], [Nagorni Karabakh, Armenia], [Chechnya, Russia], [Abkhazia, Russia]
> All recent conflicts where allegiances of minor local republics shifted from West to Russia (by will or by force).

[EU, Kazakhstan, Russia], [EU, Kazakhstan, USA]
> Kazakhstan is a major producer of natural gas, which is sold to both EU and the US by means of Russian-owned pipelines and Liquid Natural Gas (LNG) facilities.

In short—the clique algorithm produces an output that can be quickly interpreted by a human who is versed in the field.

Unfortunately, the cliques frequently overlap, and a single event or phenomena might result in multiple cliques. Other algorithms (n-clans, k_plexes, etc) exist to help solve this problem—but they are not yet implemented in NetworkX, and their implementation is beyond the scope of this book.

We will address this problem using clustering methods in the next sections.

Hierarchical Clustering

The next class of algorithms we will touch on—though briefly—is clustering algorithms. The universe of clustering algorithms is large and varied, and perhaps best addressed by other books—but I will briefly touch on the application of clustering algorithms to social network analysis and provide a quick example of useful insights that can be derived from them.

Let's first start by returning to the notion of distance. We can define distance in many ways—from geographical distance to ground travel distance to time-based distance (i.e., how long it takes to get from point A to point B), and so on. In social networks, we find two types of distance most useful; a graph distance (or path length) between pairs of nodes, and a similarity-based distance (that is, we consider nodes to be closer together if they are similar in some way).

In the Caucasus network that we used in the previous section, the graph distance matrix looks like Table 4-2.

Table 4-2. Network distances in the Caucasus network

	TR	SO	GE	IR	TK	US	AZ	CH	AR	EU	NK	KZ	RU	AB
TR	0	2	1	1	1	1	1	2	1	1	2	1	1	2
SO	2	0	2	2	2	2	2	2	2	2	3	2	1	2
GE	1	2	0	1	1	1	1	2	1	1	2	1	1	2
IR	1	2	1	0	1	2	1	2	1	1	2	1	1	2
TK	1	2	1	1	0	1	1	2	1	1	2	1	1	0
US	1	2	1	2	1	0	1	2	1	1	2	1	1	2
AZ	1	2	1	1	1	1	0	2	2	1	3	1	1	3
CH	2	2	2	2	2	2	2	0	2	2	3	2	1	2
AR	1	2	1	1	1	1	2	2	0	1	1	1	1	2
EU	1	2	1	1	1	1	1	2	1	0	2	1	1	2
NK	2	3	2	2	2	2	3	3	1	2	0	2	2	2
KZ	1	2	1	1	1	1	1	2	1	1	2	0	1	2
RU	1	1	1	1	1	1	1	1	1	1	2	1	0	1
AB	2	2	2	2	0	2	3	2	2	2	2	2	1	0

This, of course, is quite different from the geographic distances—and illustrates the fact that allegiances in the region are interleaved, with every one of the actors surrounded not by local allies, but by potential adversaries.

Let us now see if we can find the adversarial clusters in the economic network. We will use a hierarchical clustering routine in SciPy, and a snippet of code originally written by Drew Conway[16] but modified extensively for this book.

The Algorithm

Figure 4-10 shows (in a stylized way) the hierarchical clustering algorithm. The algorithm works roughly as follows:

1. Starting at the lowest level, every node is assigned its own cluster.
2. Using the distance table (Table 4-2), find the closest pair of nodes and merge them into a cluster
3. Recompute the distance table, treating the newly merged cluster as a new node.
4. Repeat steps 2 and 3, until all nodes in the network have been merged into a single large cluster (top level of the diagram).
5. Choose a useful clustering threshold between the bottom and top levels—this still requires an intervention from a human analyst and can't be automated.

16. *http://networkx.lanl.gov/examples/algorithms/blockmodel.html*

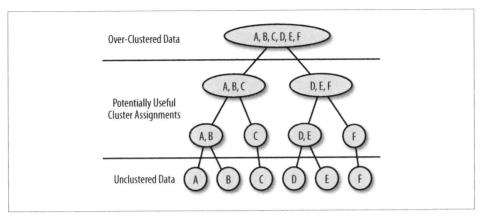

Figure 4-10. *Hierarchical clustering*

Step 3 merits further consideration. How does one go about computing the distance between a cluster a node, or between two clusters? There are three common methods for doing this:

- *Single-link*: merge two clusters with the smallest *minimum* pairwise distance
- *Average-link*: merge two clusters with the smallest *average* pairwise distance
- *Maximum-link* or *Complete-link*: merge the two clusters with the smallest *maximum* pairwise distance

The *complete-link* method is considered most sensitive to outliers, and the *single-link* method tends to form long chains of clusters that may not correspond to our intuitive understanding of what the clusters mean. *Average-link* method is considered a compromise between the two, and is in fact the most frequently used.

Clustering Cities

To better demonstrate how clustering work, let us consider a sample problem of clustering cities in the Continental U.S. The initial distance table is below; we will use single-link clustering:

	BOS	NY	DC	MIA	CHI	SEA	SF	LA	DEN
BOS	0	206	429	1504	963	2976	3095	2979	1949
NY	206	0	233	1308	802	2815	2934	2786	1771
DC	429	233	0	1075	671	2684	2799	2631	1616
MIA	1504	1308	1075	0	1329	3273	3053	2687	2037
CHI	963	802	671	1329	0	2013	2142	2054	996
SEA	2976	2815	2684	3273	2013	0	808	1131	1307
SF	3095	2934	2799	3053	2142	808	0	379	1235

	BOS	NY	DC	MIA	CHI	SEA	SF	LA	DEN
LA	2979	2786	2631	2687	2054	1131	379	0	1059
DEN	1949	1771	1616	2037	996	1307	1235	1059	0

In the first two steps, we will merge Boston, New York, and Washington, DC into a single cluster. Already, we see that the East Coast is emerging as a cluster of its own:

	BS/NY/DC	MIA	CHI	SEA	SF	LA	DEN
BS/NY/DC	0	1075	671	2684	2799	2631	1616
MIA	1075	0	1329	3273	3053	2687	2037
CHI	671	1329	0	2013	2142	2054	996
SEA	2684	3273	2013	0	808	1131	1307
SF	2799	3053	2142	808	0	379	1235
LA	2631	2687	2054	1131	379	0	1059
DEN	1616	2037	996	1307	1235	1059	0

Skipping a few more steps, Chicago joins the East Coast cluster, and San Francisco, LA, and Seattle form the West Coast cluster. Technically, Chicago and Denver should form a Midwest cluster—but since we are using the single-link distance metric, Chicago ends up being closer to the East Coast cluster than it is to Denver.

	BOS/NY/DC/CHI	MIA	SF/LA/SEA	DEN
BOS/NY/DC/CHI	0	1075	2013	996
MIA	1075	0	2687	2037
SF/LA/SEA	2013	2687	0	1059
DEN	996	2037	1059	0

This only leaves Miami and Denver unassigned. In the next steps, Denver joins Chicago in the East Coast cluster. At this point, I would argue that clustering no longer makes any sense.

The long chain reaching West from the East Coast cluster to Chicago and on to Denver is a well-known shortfall of the single-distance metric. If we were to use average-link metric in the same context, clustering would be cleaner. The tradeoff for cleaner results is a higher computational complexity—making average-link clustering unsuitable for very large datasets.

Preparing Data and Clustering

Let us now apply hierarchical clustering to the Caucasus data. First, the distance matrix needs to be computed. NetworkX provides the function to generate such a matrix—

but it is returned as a *dict of dicts*. This is a format unsuitable for further computation and needs to be moved into a SciPy matrix. Since matrices do not preserve node labels, we construct a separate array to store node labels.

Finally, we run the SciPy hierarchical clustering routines and produce the entire cluster dendrogram, reminiscent of Figure 4-10. We will need to threshold it at a certain number—here it's picked arbitrarily, but it's a parameter, so it can be easily tweaked to achieve more meaningful results.

Example 4-1. Hierarchical Clustering Algorithm

```
__author__ = """\n""".join(['Maksim Tsvetovat <maksim@tsvetovat.org',
                            'Drew Conway <drew.conway@nyu.edu>',
                            'Aric Hagberg <hagberg@lanl.gov>'])

from collections import defaultdict
import networkx as nx
import numpy
from scipy.cluster import hierarchy
from scipy.spatial import distance
import matplotlib.pyplot as plt


def create_hc(G, t=1.0):
    """
    Creates hierarchical cluster of graph G from distance matrix
    Maksim Tsvetovat ->> Generalized HC pre- and post-processing to work on labelled graphs
    and return labelled clusters
    The threshold value is now parameterized; useful range should be determined
    experimentally with each dataset
    """

    """Modified from code by Drew Conway"""

    ## Create a shortest-path distance matrix, while preserving node labels
    labels=G.nodes()
    path_length=nx.all_pairs_shortest_path_length(G)
    distances=numpy.zeros((len(G),len(G)))
    i=0
    for u,p in path_length.items():
        j=0
        for v,d in p.items():
            distances[i][j]=d
            distances[j][i]=d
            if i==j: distances[i][j]=0
            j+=1
        i+=1


    # Create hierarchical cluster
    Y=distance.squareform(distances)
    Z=hierarchy.complete(Y)  # Creates HC using farthest point linkage
    # This partition selection is arbitrary, for illustrive purposes
    membership=list(hierarchy.fcluster(Z,t=t))
```

```
# Create collection of lists for blockmodel
partition=defaultdict(list)
for n,p in zip(list(range(len(G))),membership):
    partition[p].append(labels[n])
return list(partition.values())
```

To run the `hiclus` algorithm:

```
>>> import hc
>>> hc.create_hc(eco)
[['Turkmenistan', 'Nagorni Karabakh', 'Russia', 'Abkhazia'],
['USA', 'Armenia', 'EU', 'Kazakhstan'],
['Turkey', 'Georgia', 'Iran', 'Azerbaijan'],
['Chechnya'], ['South Osetia']]
```

The result is intuitively very readable—[*Turkmenistan, Nagorni Karabakh, Russia, Abkhazia*] is a Russia-centric cluster; the [*USA, Armenia, EU, Kazakhstan*] cluster makes a lot of sense around natural gas sale and transport; and the [*Turkey, Georgia, Iran, Azerbaijan*] cluster reflects pro-Islamic and pro-Persian attitudes. Georgia is somewhat of a misfit because it is Christian and Western-allied politically—but its economic ties to Azerbaijan and Turkey are crucial and thus overshadow its Western outlook. The reset of the clustering is filled with outliers—actually, both are small countries that have caused the world quite a bit of trouble.

Block Models

A block model is a simplified network derived from the original network, where all nodes in a cluster are considered a single node, and all relationships between original nodes become aggregated into relationships between blocks.

In our sample data, a block model shows relationships between the Russia-centric, Western-oriented, and Islamic-oriented clusters (0, 1, and 2). Clusters 3 and 4 are small republics that have significant ties with Russia, but almost no ties with anyone else—due to the highly centralized nature of Russia's management of its subsidiaries.

To compute the block model, first compute and save a hierarchical clustering, then run the block model on the original graph and supply the clusters as a list of partitions. This should look something like Figure 4-11:

```
>>> clusters=hc.create_hc(eco)
>>> M=nx.blockmodel(eco,clusters)
>>> net.draw(M)
```

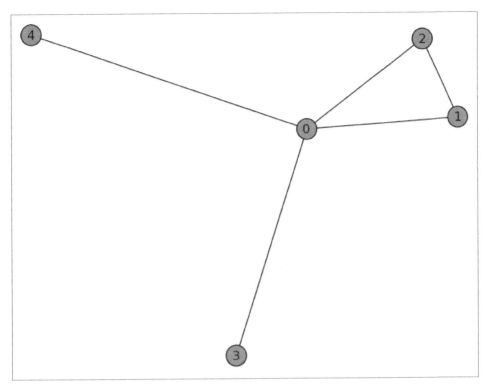

Figure 4-11. Block model of the Caucasus

A slightly more involved drawing mechanism that works on all graphs can be found in *hiclus_blockmodel.py*:

Example 4-2. Draw a network and its block model side by side

```
__author__ = """\n""".join(['Maksim Tsvetovat <maksim@tsvetovat.org',
                            'Drew Conway <drew.conway@nyu.edu>',
                            'Aric Hagberg <hagberg@lanl.gov>'])

from collections import defaultdict
import networkx as nx
import numpy
from scipy.cluster import hierarchy
from scipy.spatial import distance
import matplotlib.pyplot as plt
import hc

"""Draw a blockmodel diagram of a clustering alongside the original network"""

def hiclus_blockmodel(G):
    # Extract largest connected component into graph H
    H=nx.connected_component_subgraphs(G)[0]
    # Create paritions with hierarchical clustering
    partitions=hc.create_hc(H)
```

```
# Build blockmodel graph
BM=nx.blockmodel(H,partitions)

# Draw original graph
pos=nx.spring_layout(H,iterations=100)
fig=plt.figure(1,figsize=(6,10))
ax=fig.add_subplot(211)
nx.draw(H,pos,with_labels=False,node_size=10)
plt.xlim(0,1)
plt.ylim(0,1)

# Draw block model with weighted edges and nodes sized by
# number of internal nodes
node_size=[BM.node[x]['nnodes']*10 for x in BM.nodes()]
edge_width=[(2*d['weight']) for (u,v,d) in BM.edges(data=True)]
# Set positions to mean of positions of internal nodes from original graph
posBM={}
for n in BM:
    xy=numpy.array([pos[u] for u in BM.node[n]['graph']])
    posBM[n]=xy.mean(axis=0)
ax=fig.add_subplot(212)
nx.draw(BM,posBM,node_size=node_size,width=edge_width,with_labels=False)
plt.xlim(0,1)
plt.ylim(0,1)
plt.axis('off')
```

Triads, Network Density, and Conflict

In this chapter—actually, for all of the book so far—we have talked about uniform networks that contain one type of node, and one type of edge. However, things are about to get more interesting.

Let us suppose that instead of a single link type we now have two—friendship and conflict. We will also introduce some dynamics, on both the dyadic and triadic level.

We have all witnessed social turmoil—or even have been involved in the midst of it. A long-married couple decides to divorce, and suddenly their friends are faced with difficult decisions. They may feel pressured to side with one partner or the other, potentially splitting long-standing friendships and dividing a formerly cohesive network into "his side" and "her side." As the wounds of the split-up heal, the space is opened up for creation of new friendships and romantic relationships, and the cycle starts again.

We can model this process using a few very simple rules:

Ordered

1. Friend of my friend is my friend (close a structural hole)
2. Enemy of my friend is my enemy (achieve a balanced triad)
3. Friend of my enemy is my enemy
4. Enemy of my enemy is my friend

Actually, rules 2,3, and 4 all describe the same (undirected) triad, just from a different point of view; we'll call them all "Rule 2" (Figure 4-12). These rules are, in fact, some of the first attempts to describe social complexity in the history of civilization; the first written mention of these rules is in the Bible (*Exodus 23:22*, with a number of other mentions).

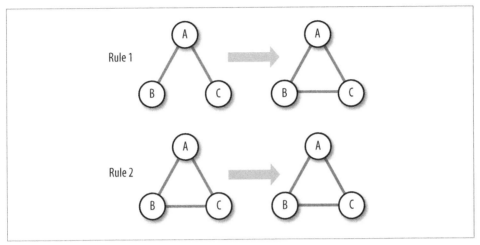

Figure 4-12. Rules for change in triads (with conflict)

Let's start with the behavior of a social network without either Rule 1 or Rule 2: if we start with a set of unconnected nodes and connect them randomly at a constant, we will at the end receive a simple random graph with a normal distribution of node degrees (an *Erdos* random graph). The density of the network (i.e., the number of connections vs. number of possible connections) will rise until every node is connected to every other node (a *complete graph* or a *clique*). This, of course, is not terribly interesting.

Let us now turn on Rule 1. If an open triad A→B→C is detected, with some probability we will also add a link A→ C. We are still adding links randomly, so at first, the network will grow linearly. At a certain point, a *critical mass* of connection has been created, and every new connection is likely to create an open triad. This open triad is then closed by Rule 1, which may in turn create more open triads, which then get closed, and so on.

In a sense, the network passes from a linear growth to an exponential growth. It *goes viral!* (Figure 4-13) The density of connections increases rapidly, until no new connections can be made and we have a complete graph. Of course, in reality, there is a limit to the number of possible connections in the network, a *saturation density*. This density can be a property of the network itself, or the environment in which the network is developing—or a result of Rule 2 (as in our system).

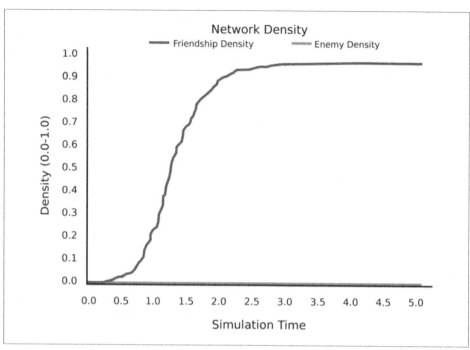

Figure 4-13. Closing the triads—Rule 1 activated

Conflict is introduced in the network at a constant probability, by changing a single friendship tie into an enemy tie. What happens then is illustrated in Figure 4-14. In this simple example, a network consisting of 4 closed triads is struck by a conflict on a single edge. Triad A–B–C becomes unbalanced due to a conflict between B and C; thus A is forced to take sides in the conflict by choosing to remain friends with either B or C, at random. Adding conflict to the A–C edge forces another triad (A–C–D) to become unbalanced, thus drawing agent D into the conflict. If agent D then chooses to isolate C from the rest of the network, the propagation of the conflict can be stopped. However, if instead it separates from A, this will cause the conflict to propagate further and destroy more links. Having more ties increases an agent's probability of forming even more ties, but also increases the probability that a conflict between two agents will spread throughout the network (Figure 4-14).

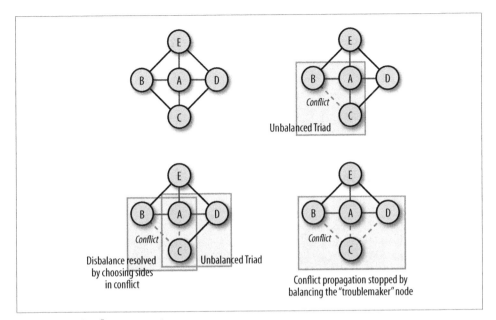

Figure 4-14. Conflict propagation

As a result, network density no longer grows to near 100%; but instead, once it reaches a second *critical mass* value, conflicts become more prominent (as can be seen in Figure 4-15) and bring the network density back down. This kind of behavior is called *self-organized criticality*—my model provides just a simple way to generate such effects in social networks. This is in a way similar to forest fires: the denser the forest, the more likely it is that the next fire will be catastrophic—permitting smaller fires down-regulates the density of the forest to a level where most fires are relatively well-contained.

We will talk more about dynamics of social networks in Chapter 6—but, meanwhile, it is time to start looking at social network data with many different types of nodes—data that can better approximate what we know about social networks.

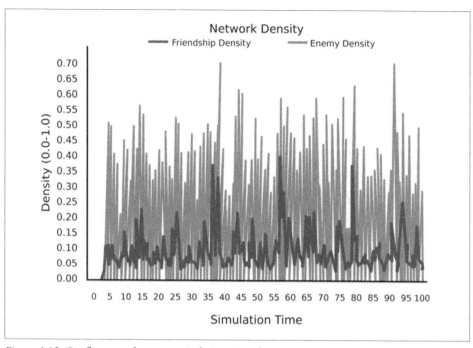

Figure 4-15. Conflict cascades occur—Rule 2 activated

## CHAPTER 5

2-Mode Networks

In this chapter, we will explore ways of analyzing complex networks with two or more different types of nodes. But first, as usual, we will lead off with a story.

Does Campaign Finance Influence Elections?

"We have the best government that money can buy," said Mark Twain.

Every April in Chicago's Palmer House Hilton, political scientists square off at the Midwest Political Science Association conference (the top venue for discussing special-interest group politics and campaign finance) and debate whether Mark Twain was right, or whether the American system, in fact, is immune to the influence of money.

We[1] entered this fray in 2006, bringing with us a large-scale social network study of campaign finance and its influence on electoral outcome. In this section, we'll give an overview of this study, and delve into the methods used to derive the results.

But first, let's play a little game.

Take a look at Figure 5-1. Every node on this chart is a political organization or political action committee (PAC) actively involved in the 2000 congressional and presidential elections. Red and blue nodes, respectively, are Republican and Democratic committees (national and state), green nodes are single-issue groups, purple nodes are industry associations, and yellow are non-profit organizations. The links between PACs are determined by where their money is spent—if PAC-A and PAC-B route donations to the same candidates, they become linked—and the more they have in common, the stronger this link becomes. The strongest links are shown with thicker lines on the diagram (we will go over the details of how this is done a little bit later).

---

1. Suzanne McDonald and Max Tsvetovat

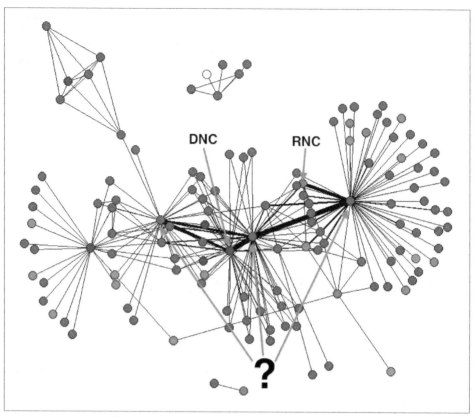

Figure 5-1. Campaign finance—the network of Political Action Committees (PACs)

This study was based on data released by the Federal Election Commission, pursuant to the McCain-Finegold Campaign Finance Act.[2] The data is based on forms that PACs are required to file every time they make a campaign contribution to a candidate. The data is still available for every election year at *http://fec.gov/*, but the quality of the information and amount of coverage varies depending on the political environment of the day.

As you can see, the single-issue PACs dominate the picture. On the right is the Republican cluster, led by the Republican National Committee (RNC), and on the left is the Democratic cluster and the Democratic National Committee (DNC). However, right next to the "official players," connected to them with thickest links, are three PACs that seem to wield a significant amount of power in the network.

Can anyone guess what they are?

2. The Citizens United decision by the Supreme Court has seriously undermined our ability to study these sort of interactions in the future; much of the data has become unavailable in 2010.

The answers are shown in Figure 5-2. The nodes on the left and right of the strong-link triads are, in turn, NARAL (National Abortion and Reproductive Rights Action League), and the National Right to Life PAC—representing the two sides of the abortion issue, which, in 2000 as well as now, is one of the most divisive issues in American politics.

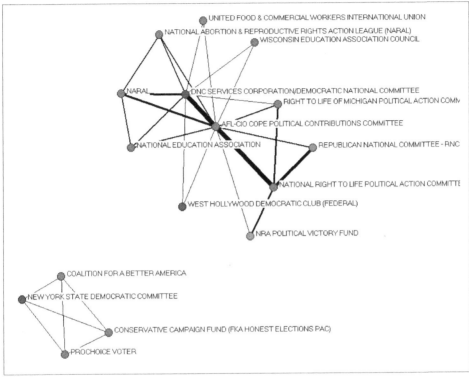

Figure 5-2. Campaign finance—the network of Political Action Committees (core network)

In the middle is the AFL-CIO Political Action Committee, representing America's largest labor union and, by proxy, over 11 million voters. The union vote historically tended to be Democratic, but Republicans needed to win key industrial states such as Ohio and Michigan in order to gain control of Congress and elect a Republican president—and that meant peeling union vote away from its traditional constituency. This required a "fulcrum issue": an issue that was divisive enough to make union members break with their party affiliation—and abortion was it.

Whether this was by design or by accident of fate, we can now state that abortion was one of the few issues swaying the 2000 election, if not *the* decisive issue.[3]

For an extra bit of amusement, I'd like to direct your attention to the bottom-left corner of Figure 5-2. This entire cluster of PACs (except from NY DNC) were formed for one reason only—to defeat Hillary Clinton.

We will come back to the campaign data in a little bit, but first, let's talk about how these kinds of studies can be done.

Theory of 2-Mode Networks

Much of network data currently available comes in a *2-mode* (or bimodal, or bipartite) format—that is, there are two different types of nodes, and links determine relationships between one set of nodes and the other.

For example, a dataset can contain data on political contributions (*PAC* contributing to a *Candidate*); employment (*People* employed by *Organizations*); or social media (*People* liking *Pages*). Frequently, these networks contain more than two types of nodes —for example, *angel investors* investing in *companies* founded by *people* (this is made even more interesting because successful company founders eventually become angel investors themselves). However, the methodology remains roughly the same.

Sociologists recognize a concept called *duality* of persons and groups.[4] Essentially, what this means is that people's ideas, attitudes, and social connections are shaped by membership in groups, and groups are shaped by the attitudes of their members. This applies to corporations, gangs, political parties, social clubs, and so on. Since people are seldom members of only one group, comembership can be viewed as a way to analyze and aggregate similarities and differences between individuals.

Affiliation Networks

Figure 5-3 shows a simple 2-mode network—persons A and B are both members of a club. Essentially they form an open triad, or a structural hole—but we can infer that if A and B are members of the same club, they may know each other; and thus infer that the triad is indeed closed. This, of course, is a fairly weak inference: to make a more concrete case, one must consider if they were members of the club at the same time, or if the club has multiple chapters in different cities, etc. But it's a start.

---

3. For a more detailed explanation, see Robbins, S. and M. Tsvetovat, "Guns, Babies, and Labor: Networks of Money in the 2000 Elections". Presented at the 66th Annual Meeting of the Midwest Political Science Association, Chicago, IL, 2008.

4. Breiger, Ronald. "Duality of Persons and Groups". *Social Forces* 53 (1974).

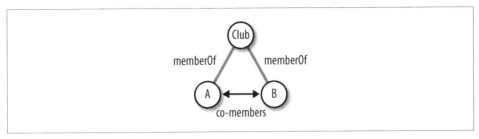

Figure 5-3. Triadic closure and comembership

Now imagine that the same people are members of more than one club (as shown in the top of Figure 5-4, where nodes E, F, and H are comembers in 2 clubs). This presents a stronger association between the people, perhaps hinting at a common group identity. We can continue to accumulate comemberships until we can be fairly certain the connections are real, and weigh the inferred links accordingly.

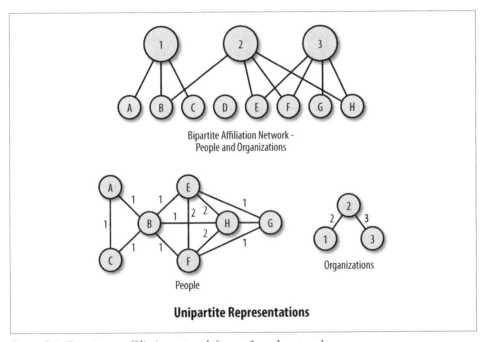

Figure 5-4. Creating an affiliation network from a 2-mode network

Figure 5-4 shows two resulting projected networks—a network of people where links were determined through comembership in groups, and a network of groups where links were determined by comembership of people. To create these networks, we simply count the comemberships for every one of the people—or, alternatively, for every one of the clubs.

These networks can be treated with the same sort of analyses as any other social network —but are particularly well-suited for analysis with the *island method* ("Islands in the Net" on page 62) and *clustering* ("Hierarchical Clustering" on page 81) techniques. This is due to the fact that these networks are essentially networks of similarities or correlations, so meaning can be easily discerned.

Attribute Networks

Another application of 2-mode network analysis is based on the idea of *homophily* (Greek, "love of the similar")—the idea that people who share interests or attributes are more likely to talk to each other and form ties than people who are very different. What about "opposites attract" and other bits of lore? The theory seems to stand in some cases, and fails in some others, so it's not universal by any means. We also know that as people become more tightly connected, they become more similar in their views —but up to a certain limit.

However, if one wants to build a "suggest a friend" mechanism for their online social network, treating an attribute or interest matrix as a 2-mode network can be a useful mechanism. All one has to do is treat every one of the pieces of information (tags, keywords, etc.) as a node in a 2-mode network, compute a person-to-person affiliation network from it, and apply the island method or clustering to find potential groupings of people. Then, to suggest friends, simply pick the top links in the affiliation network.

An inverse affiliation network—attributes through people—could provide very interesting insights as well. Let's suppose that we are interested in mapping political discourse on Twitter. We harvest tweets from several thousand people containing the hashtag #*election*, build a 2-mode network from people to hashtags, and compute a hashtag-through-people affiliation network. In such networks, clusters will act as proxies for entire areas of discourse—and will likely separate liberal and conservative Twitter users. Further exploration of clusters may yield an idea of divisions inside the two major parties, such as the emergence of the Tea Party as an independent entity, and its later reabsorption into mainstream Republican discourse.

A Little Math

Let us express a sample network as an adjacency matrix ("Adjacency Matrices" on page 21):

```
   1 2 3 4 5
A  0 0 0 0 1
B  1 0 0 0 0
C  1 1 0 0 0
D  0 1 1 1 1
E  0 0 1 0 0
F  0 0 1 1 0
```

Now, let us compare nodes *D* and *F*; we can do this by multiplying their rows in the table bit by bit:

```
       1 2 3 4 5    Sum
    D  0 1 1 1 1   = 4
    F  0 0 1 1 0   = 4
  D*F  0 0 1 1 0   = 2
```

D and F have 2 edges in common. Let us now repeat this for every pair of nodes, and place them in a matrix like this:

```
   A B C D E F
A  0 0 0 1 0 0
B  0 0 1 0 0 0
C  0 1 0 1 0 0
D  1 0 1 0 1 2
E  0 0 0 1 0 1
F  0 0 0 2 1 0
```

The resulting adjacency matrix represents the affiliation network of nodes A-F—and the operation is none other then *matrix multiplication*. In this exercise, we multiplied the adjacency matrix A by its transposed version (A^t): $AA=A^*A^T$.

 In this book, we will use a mathematically less rigorous, but more readable notation: a 2-mode network containing, for example, *People* and *Clubs* will be called *PC*; its derivative network connecting *People* with other *People* nodes will be called *PP*, etc.

This computation may take quite some time. In fact, the computational complexity of this operation is $O(n^*m^*n)$ where *n* is the "outer dimension" (*pacs* in this case), and *m* is the "inner dimension" of the multiplication. Thus, computing a projected 1-mode network from a 10×5 2-mode network would take $10^*5^*10=500$ operations on the "long side," and $5^*10^*5=250$ operations on the "short side." In this case, an operation involves looking up the value of a single edge (a, b) given 2 nodes—and if this operation involves text matching, the computation of projected networks can become very computationally expensive. Smart indexing (e.g., using Python dicts or SQL indexes) can make this operation near-instant, and reduce time to compute projected networks by an order of 2 or 3.

 If you have not been previously exposed to matrix algebra (which I admit is rather dry despite its usefulness), a useful way to think about matrix multiplication is this: if we multiply *CP* by *PC*, the internal dimensions (P) must be the same. The internal dimension will "cancel out", leaving us with matrix *CC*. What does AB * BC * CD * DA equal? AB * BC = AC; AC * CD = AD; AD * DA == AA; we have gone a full circle. This ability to create long multiplication sequences will become highly useful in "Expanding Multimode Networks" on page 105.

2-Mode Networks in Practice

NetworkX provides a number of functions for working with 2-mode networks. To use these functions, make sure that your installation of NetworkX is version 1.5 or newer. Let us try a simple example.

The data we'll use is a small subset of the campaign finance data we talked about earlier. The original dataset included over 500,000 transactions; we will only look at a few hundred. In the example, every PAC and every candidate are assigned an ID; in fact, these are unique IDs assigned by the Federal Election Committee. The candidate ID is actually *somewhat* human-readable. For example, candidate H6IL14095 is running for the (H)ouse in (IL)linois, in the 14th district—enough information to find out that his name is Dennis Hastert (Rep). FEC also provides a comprehensive database of all candidates (up to their home addresses), [5] but we shall refrain from cyber-stalking in this book.

The data file we are going to use is in the CSV (comma-separated value) format (Table 5-1), and includes a number of values that we need, and a number of things we will disregard for now. Column 1 is the FEC ID of the PAC, Column 13 contains the ID of the candidate receiving the contribution, and Column 11 contains the amount of the contribution. The format may have changed between 2000 and now, but remains fairly similar; you should have no problems modifying the code below to work on current data.

```
import csv
import math
import networkx as net

## Import bi-partite (bi-modal) functions
from networkx.algorithms import bipartite as bi

## Read the data from a CSV file
## We use the Universal new-line mode since many CSV files are created with Excel
r=csv.reader(open('campaign_short.csv','rU'))

## 2-mode graphs are usually directed. Here, their direction implies money flow
g=net.Graph()

## we need to keep track separately of nodes of all types
pacs=[]
candidates=[]

## Construct a directed graph from edges in the CSV file
for row in r:
    if row[0] not in pacs:
        pacs.append(row[0])
    if row[12] not in candidates:
        candidates.append(row[12])
    g.add_edge(row[0],row[12], weight=int(row[10]))
```

5. *http://fec.gov/finance/disclosure/ftp_download.shtml*

Table 5-1. Campaign finance transaction log—first 20 lines

Source ID				Tax ID	Org. Type	Month	Day	Cent.	Yr	Amount	Other ID	Candidate ID	Trans. ID
C0000042	N	MY	P	99034551644	24K	2	8	19	99	0001000	C00319285	S4M000037	175211
C0000042	N	MY	P	99034551644	24K	5	20	19	99	0001250	C00208090	H6IL14095	175212
C0000042	N	MY	P	99034551644	24K	5	20	19	99	0001000	C00013573	H6IL06026	175213
C0000042	N	MY	P	99034551644	24K	5	20	19	99	0001000	C00079020	H8IL10016	175214
C0000042	N	Q1	G	2035433084	24K	3	28	20	0	0002500	C00350785	H0IL10120	946633
C0000042	N	Q1	P	2035433084	24K	2	15	20	0	0001000	C00350785	H0IL10120	946634
C0000042	N	Q1	G	2035433084	24K	3	28	20	0	0001000	C00346759	H8CT05104	946635
C0000042	N	Q1	P	2035433084	24K	3	13	20	0	0000500	C00257121	H2IL01042	946636
C0000042	N	Q1	P	2035433084	24K	2	17	20	0	0000500	C00350496	H0IL15061	946637
C0000042	N	Q2	G	2035834069	24K	6	5	20	0	0001000	C00303354	S4MI00165	1258632
C0000042	N	Q2	G	2035834069	24K	6	5	20	0	0002000	C00309930	H6IL17106	1258633
C0000042	N	Q2	G	2035834069	24K	6	5	20	0	0000500	C00253930	H2WI05150	1258634
C0000042	N	Q2	G	2035834069	24K	6	5	20	0	0000500	C00237198	H0OH08029	1258635
C0000042	N	Q2	G	2035834069	24K	6	5	20	0	0001000	C00327874	H8WI00026	1258636
C0000042	N	Q2	G	2035834069	24K	6	5	20	0	0000500	C00343608	H4PA13066	1258637
C0000042	N	Q2	G	2035834069	24K	6	5	20	0	0003000	C00208090	H6IL14095	1258638
C0000042	N	Q2	G	2035834070	24K	6	5	20	0	0000500	C00198614	H0MD08021	1258639
C0000042	N	Q2	G	2035834070	24K	6	5	20	0	0000500	C00301622	H6KY03090	1258640
C0000042	N	Q2	G	2035834070	24K	6	5	20	0	0000500	C00349431	H0MT00033	1258641
C0000042	N	Q2	G	2035834070	24K	6	5	20	0	0000500	C00336065	H8NY27077	1258642

PAC Networks

Now we have constructed a graph object—what can we do with it? Let's start by computing an affiliation network of the PACs:

```
pacnet=bi.weighted_projected_graph(g, pacs, ratio=False)
```

The network has a connected component and a couple isolates. These are artifacts of when we wantonly chopped off a piece of a dataset for use as an example—and we can throw them away here just as well, by taking only the largest connected component:

```
pacnet=net.connected_component_subgraphs(pacnet)[0]
```

We would like to plot the resulting network and highlight strength of relationships using color and edge thickness. Since edge value will vary widely, it is wise to take use its logarithm to compress the numeric range:

```
weights=[math.log(edata['weight']) for f,t,edata in pacnet.edges(data=True)]
```

Finally, we draw the graph:

```
net.draw_networkx(p,width=weights, edge_color=weights)
```

The resulting picture should be somewhat similar to Figure 5-5. Thick red lines signify strong relationships; in this dataset the strongest relationship is between ID C00000422, a certain Dr. Craig Anderson of Columbus, OH; and ID C00000372: Maintenance of Way Political League, a railroad employees union PAC located in Southfield, Michigan.

Candidate Networks

To compute the candidate network, we shall simply reverse the direction of projection —and compute a projected graph on the *candidates* table rather than the *pacs* table:

```
cannet=bi.weighted_projected_graph(g, candidates, ratio=False)
cannet=net.connected_component_subgraphs(cannet)[0]
weights=[math.log(edata['weight']) for f,t,edata in cannet.edges(data=True)]
net.draw_networkx(cannet,width=weights, edge_color=weights)
```

The resulting network is significantly larger and will take a long time to draw; it will also look something like a hairball.[6] It is clear that the network has a number of distinct clusters; we will now try to find them using the *island method* from "Islands in the Net" on page 62. First, let's look at the histogram of edge values—this will help us determine where to place the "water level". Figure 5-6 shows that approximately 80% of edges are weighted below 0.9, so we can safely remove them:

---

6. This is a proper scientific term!

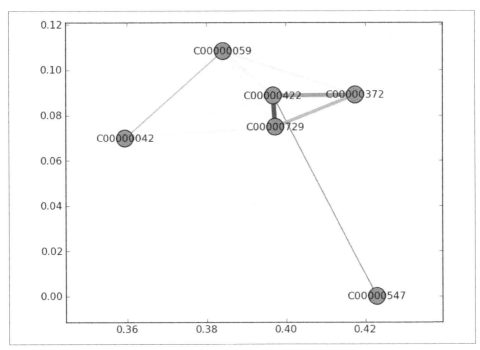

Figure 5-5. Sample affiliation network of PACs

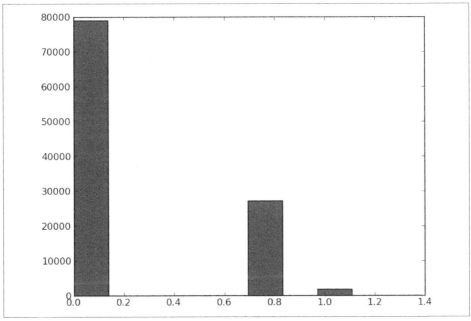

Figure 5-6. Network of Congressional candidates—edge weight histogram

```
def trim_edges(g, weight=1):
    g2=net.Graph()
    for f, to, edata in g.edges(data=True):
        if edata['weight'] > weight:
            g2.add_edge(f,to,edata)
    return g2

plot.hist(weights)

## The weights histogram is logarithmic;
## we should compute the original weight = e^log_weight
cannet_trim=trim_edges(cannet, weight=math.exp(0.9))

## re-calculate weights based on the new graph
weights=[edata['weight'] for f,t,edata in cannet_trim.edges(data=True)]
net.draw_networkx(cannet_trim,width=weights, edge_color=weights)
```

The core network (Figure 5-7) clearly contains a number of cohesive clusters that are connected by boundary spanner candidates. In 2000, many Democrats tended to be conservative—and as a result, received a lot of funding from normally Republican backers. This, or course, didn't stop them from losing the election.

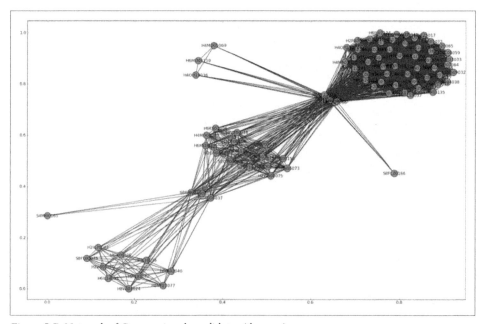

Figure 5-7. Network of Congressional candidates (the core)

From this point on, we can use hierarchical clustering (see "Hierarchical Clustering" on page 81) to determine who is in these clusters. Boundary spanners can be found using betweenness centrality ("Find the Communication Bottlenecks and/or Community Bridges" on page 51) or triad census ("Analyzing Triads in Real Networks" on page 77). Since these techniques have been already explained in previous chapters, we shall leave this as an exercise to the reader.[7]

Expanding Multimode Networks

In the previous section, we talked about working with 2-mode networks. However, we all realize that the world is even more complex and the number of types of nodes and edges in a network can be quite large. Thankfully, the technique we discussed in the previous section can be easily extended to any network-oriented data model. One just has to be careful to keep track of what each network and projected network actually means—and not get lost in the sea of matrix multiplications.

As an example, we'd like to offer a data model of an organization, adapted from the work of David Krackhardt and Kathleen Carley.[8]

Let us imagine ACME, Inc., a small company that makes widgets. A number of people are working for this company, with some kind of a *chain of command*. These people have *friendships* inside and outside the firm, have a formal education in some field of *knowledge*, and possess certain *resources*. The widgets that the company makes consist of *parts* or *tasks*, with each of the tasks requiring somebody to apply a skill to a resource (i.e., to make a sprocket, a *person* who *knows* how to operate a *lathe* and has some *steel* must spend some time making sprockets.)

Did you see all of the italicized words? All of these can be considered *nodes* in a multimode network sense, and from this we can build a social-network representation of ACME's world, something similar to Figure 5-8. The entity-relationship diagram shows that with only four entities in the mix, the relationship map can become quite complex. In this example, we won't address all of the possible relationships—but we'll show how to derive new inferences and the rest will fall into place.

---

7. In 1966, Marvin Minsky (the father of artificial intelligence) assigned computer vision as an undergrad summer project. This shouldn't be nearly as difficult.

8. Krackhardt, David, and Kathleen Carley. "A PCANS Model of Structure in Organizations". Proceedings of the 1998 International Symposium on Command and Control Research and Technology. In this book, we use a different notation to keep it consistent with the rest of the text.

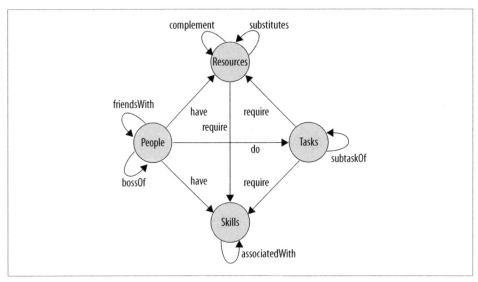

Figure 5-8. Entity-relationship diagram of a simple organization

In a matrix form, the organizational model would look like Table 5-2.

Table 5-2. Entities and relationships as an adjacency matrix

	People	Skills	Resources	Tasks
People	PP: Who knows whom?	PS: Who knows what?	PR: Who has what?	PT: Who does what?
Skills		SS: What skills go together?	SR: What skills are needed for a resource?	ST: What skills are needed for a task?
Resources			RR: What resources go together?	RT: What resources are needed for a task?
Task				TT: What is the task precedence?

Each of the matrices are simply a table where (for example) one would record how much a certain Joe knows about operating a lathe (skill table) or whether Joe has any metal to make sprockets.

We can now treat each one just like a bipartite network in the previous section. Unfortunately, NetworkX does not provide an extended functionality for multipartite networks, so we will have to drop down to the matrix level to make these computations:

```
import numpy as num

pc=net.adj_matrix(g) #get an adjacency matrix from a network
cp = pc.transpose() #make a transposed matrix
```

```
cc= pc*cp # compute a PAC-to-PAC network
cc_graph = net.Graph(cc) #re-create a NetworkX object from an adjacency matrix
```

Now let's have some fun with this. Since we can perform infinitely long sequences of matrix multiplications to suit our needs, we can make long-ranging inferences on this data. For example:

- PP * PP = PP: The new network means "who are friends-of-friends?"
- PT * PT^t = PT * TP = PP: this means: "who is working together, and on how many tasks?"
- PT * TT = PT: For each person, what tasks are in their critical path?
- TT * TT = TT: Interdependent tasks
- PT * TT * TP = PP: What people are in a person's critical path?
- PT * TT * TT' * TP = PP: Who is working together on concurrent tasks?

Exercise

In this model, how do you determine what tasks are feasible? Let us assume that a task can be done if a person assigned to do the task has the resources required for completing the task.

The equation RT^t * PR^t = TR * RP = TP represents tasks that *can be done* by a person.

The equation TP * PT = TT will produce a matrix. The diagonal of this matrix represents how many possible ways there are to accomplish a task. If the number is 0, a task is not feasible.

An entire field of computational organization theory has grown around this type of model. The simulation of terrorist networks in the beginning of the book is built upon similar principles (but on a much more advanced level), as well as many other models, both static and dynamic. The resource allocation and feasibility calculations are now part of Microsoft Project.

There is one caveat if any of you would like to use this in consulting practice. No business, no matter now well-run, will ever have a complete picture of its business model, its social network, and the knowledge embedded in its employee's minds. Some might try to actively engineer a company to conform to an organizational model—but, as we mentioned in the conversation about informal networks, this will be immediately circumvented by an informal structure.

## CHAPTER 6

Going Viral! Information Diffusion

This chapter is probably why you picked up this book in the first place. Many people wonder how things (videos, sites, news, and so on) "go viral" online—diffuse rapidly and become a part of the culture (and in the process, make their authors rich). We should forewarn you that we have no ready-made recipe. Nobody really has a recipe, and there is a fair bit of luck involved—but in this chapter we'll try to get you closer to understanding what drives diffusion and how your decisions can drive adoption of a product.

Anatomy of a Viral Video

Let us suppose that you made a really cute video of your cat, posted it on YouTube and Tweeted about it. Are you on your way to riches? Well, it depends.

It largely depends on who sees it and what they do with it afterwards. At first, the only people that see it are in your immediate *ego network*—i.e., your friends. As such, growth in the number of views is very slow; it is linear over time, meaning that views happen at a constant rate. In this case, we can describe the number of views as a Poisson process, where every act of viewing your cat video is independent of every other act. At the end, the total number of views you would get would be mathematically related to the number of followers you have—your *degree centrality*.

But if something else happens and your friends retweet the video to their friends (and so on, exposing more and more people to it), your cat is suddenly in the most popular video on YouTube, and Hollywood producers come knocking at your door. Or maybe not.

A very curious thing happens somewhere in the middle of the process. One of your friends says "have you seen this video?" and the other replies "yes, I already have"— and this reinforces the idea that the video constitutes a *meme*, a new cultural artifact that stands on its own. Suddenly, exposing others to the meme becomes second nature or even a required action.

The qualitative shift from a thing that doesn't matter (but is cute or interesting) to a "must share" is a sharp inflection that in the adoption curve, otherwise known as *critical mass*. If the meme fails to reach critical mass within a certain amount of time, its adoption rate starts falling and it eventually dies.

If, however, critical mass is reached, it will grow exponentially until it reaches *saturation point*—i.e., almost everyone that could have adopted the meme has already done so. From that point, the meme will decline.

An important note is that the notions of critical mass and saturation apply to every network or community—it is possible for a meme to reach saturation point in one community and be virtually unknown in another. However, since communities are interlinked, it is possible for a meme to jump to a new community via *boundary spanners*, and find a new critical mass and an even higher saturation point.

What Did Facebook Do Right?

Before there was Facebook, there were other social networks. Some of us still have MySpace accounts. Some remember Friendster. But before Friendster, before all others, there was SixDegrees. SixDegrees was launched in 1997[1] and promised to connect people to their friends, and, among their friends, the best lawyers, doctors, plumbers, etc. By doing so, it would fulfill the useful function of helping people accomplish tasks via their social network.

SixDegrees launched about 5 years before its time, and never reached critical mass, despite a national ad campaign, good design (for 1997), good presence in the blogs (the venerable Slashdot and BoingBoing both did features on it) and magazines (Wired).

What went wrong? The answer is really quite simple—SixDegrees never reached critical mass. They launched nationally and attempted to build an essentially local marketplace that spanned the entire country, and as a result failed to fulfill their task—it was nearly impossible to actually find a plumber on the site, partially because few plumbers had Internet access at the time (or bothered to create an online presence), and partially because the actual connection density was extremely low.

When Facebook launched in 2003 (under the original name of "Facemash"), it was confined to a small dense community—Harvard undergraduates. Launching in a confined space allowed them to reach critical mass quickly. In fact, within approximately 4 hours from its launch, the site attracted 450 visitors, or about 6% of the total undergraduate population. Remember the number 6%; it's important.

Within Harvard, early Facebook went through a number of iterations until arriving at a fairly scalable design and eventually reached saturation at about 50% of Harvard undergrads. From there, its reach was expanded to other Ivy league schools, one by

1. That's, like, the last century.

one, and eventually to all universities in the US. Finally, in 2005, it was opened to high-school students—and the stage for world domination was set.

The rule that Facebook followed—and what made it different from SixDegrees and Friendster—was to achieve saturation within a community before moving to a larger community. This way, critical mass was never lost and new members folded neatly into the social structure set up by their peers from other schools.

How Do You Estimate Critical Mass?

In "Triads, Network Density, and Conflict" on page 88, we talked about propagation of conflict in social networks and its effect on the density of ties in the network. If you go back and look closely at Figure 4-13, you will see a very similar growth function—the same *sigmoid* shape as we observe in Figure 6-1.

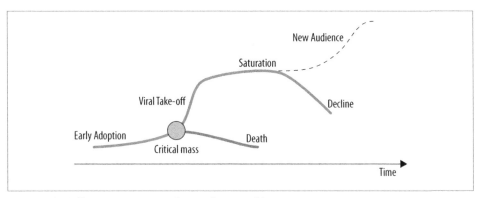

Figure 6-1. Diffusion curve—critical mass, boom and bust

If the transition from linear propagation to exponential (viral) growth indeed depends on triadic closure (i.e., "friend of a friend is my friend"),[2] then the critical mass of connections can be estimated by measuring the probability that a randomly created link from A to B will form one or more open triads with other nodes. This is proportional to the number of nodes already connected(we double the number of nodes because each tie involves 2 nodes):

P(open_triad) ~= #ties/(2*#nodes)

Thus, probability of an open triad reaches 50% when a quarter of the nodes are connected—and every new connection causes the triadic closure rules to create even more connections, further increasing the probability of a cascade.

---

2. This is our theory, supported by a number of scholarly papers—but so far there is no universally accepted theory in the field. Your mileage may vary.

In our experiments, we have found that the transition from linear growth (where connections are added one by one) to going viral happens somewhere around 7% density —i.e., if 7% of people in the intended audience adopt a meme, retweet a video, join a site, etc., the rest will follow shortly in a viral wave.

This was the "magic number" that pushed Facebook over the edge at Harvard, and in the course of our research, we have collected a number of other examples that went viral below the 10% saturation mark.

A corollary to this is that it's much easier to achieve critical mass in a smaller community —which Mark Zuckerberg either understood instinctively or (more likely) stumbled upon by accident.

 To a founder of a startup, this is counterintuitive. Every venture capitalist wants to know how big the overall market is, and the startup's plans for achieving market penetration. Going after small, self-contained market niches seems to defeat the purpose of exponential growth. However, high saturation in a niche is a good springboard to other niches—whether they are geographically close or unite people by interest.

Wikinomics of Critical Mass

There is one more consideration to the critical mass question—the idea of cost of participation. Even in the world of free services, everything has a cost. It could be a monetary cost, a time cost, or an opportunity cost (i.e., time spent on Facebook is not time spent in a bar—at least until mobile phones became ubiquitous). Other forms of participatory culture such as Wikipedia demand even higher time investments of its authors and editors, while the benefits remain ephemeral.

An outdated yet potent example of this is the advent of the fax machine. When the first fax machine rolled off the Xerox assembly line in the mid-1970s, it cost several thousand dollars, and was *utterly and completely useless*. After all, if a fax was sent from it, there was no machine on the other end to receive it. When the 2nd fax machine rolled off a few minutes later, the value of both increased infinitely—now a bank could communicate with its branch office. However, the usefulness of the machine kept increasing as more and more machines were produced, until the fax machine became an indispensable business tool.

In the case of fax machines, the original application was to connect branch offices of large companies with headquarters (replacing bulky telex machines), so each company reached its own critical mass of adoption independently and on its own timeline—but given considerable investment into equipment, it would have been very difficult or impossible to sell the idea of a fax machine on the grander scale.

An economist could talk about these ideas in terms of transaction costs, and draw curves that look somewhat like Figure 6-2.

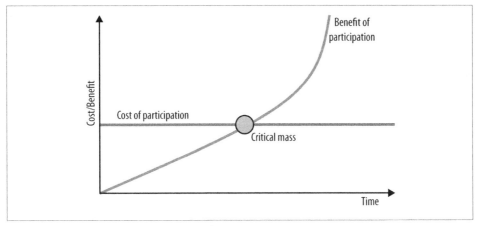

Figure 6-2. Cost curve—economics of social media

Let us imagine that the cost of participation remains constant. In some cases (e.g., fax machines), the cost goes down as the equipment becomes more mass-produced, but in participatory culture (e.g., Wikipedia), the cost actually goes up—but we can consider it constant in the short term.

To an early adopter, the cost is very real and the benefit is yet to materialize. As more people join the network, the benefit rises as a function of number of connections, making the new idea or meme or social network site an easier sell every step of the way.

Critical mass will be reached when the benefits of using the product start outweighing the cost; at this point, each connection will in turn breed more connections, further increasing the benefit—while the cost still remains constant.

If the cost/benefit crossover is never reached, it may not matter how many connections are in the network—eventually the network will fail.

Content is (Still) King

When I started working on Web projects in 1995,[3] we used to have a saying: "Content is King." That is what drove users to the site, made them stay there, and come back. Many theories proliferated at the time—ideas that it should not take more than 6 clicks for a user to find what he wants, and that important information should never be hidden "below the cut" (off the screen when the page first loads). These are good design principles, then and now. However, if the site's content was compelling, none of that mattered. People clicked and scrolled if the prize was worth it in the end.

---

3. Yes, I'm old.

The idea is the same today: if content is compelling in one way or another, this raises the benefit and makes the cost-benefit crossover happen sooner, thus shifting the critical mass of connections down from 7% to 3% or 4%. If the content quality is not very good, however, critical mass may not be reachable at all.

This is where quantitative analysis of social networks stops, and theories of what makes messages compelling proliferate out of control. The theory below is one of many possible ways of explaining information diffusion qualitatively.

When we would like to know if a message will diffuse through a network, what we are really asking is "will this message resonate with the members of the network?". Or, more exactly, "how will individuals receive the message?". We can break down the effect of the message into a number of variables:

Relevance
>   Do I care at all? (And its variant, *Saliency*—do I care right now?)

Resonance
>   Does the content of the message mesh with what I already believe in?

Severity
>   How good or bad is the content of the message?

Immediacy
>   Does this message demand an immediate action? Combined with *Severity*, what is the consequence of inaction?

Certainty
>   Does the effect of this message cause certain pain or pleasure or is the chance low?

Source
>   Who did this message come from and do I trust this person? Has it been corroborated by someone else?

Entertainment value
>   Is it funny? A good read?

Heterogenous Preferences

The evaluation I showed in the previous section applies to a specific message (m) and a specific person (P). However, every person receiving the message is likely to grade it in their own idiosyncratic ways. Aggregation of heterogenous personal preferences is a hard problem in economics. To simplify this very complex problem, let us suppose that all of the above variables can be written as numbers (let's say 0 through 1). Then, each message can be evaluated as:

$$v_m = \beta_1 Relevance + \beta_2 Resonance + \beta_3 Severity + ... + \beta_7 Entertainment$$

$$\beta_1 + \beta_2 + ... + \beta_7 = 1$$

The beta values symbolize importance of each of the factors to adoption of a message, for a specific individual. Thus, some people are highly vulnerable to scare tactics (messages with high immediacy and severity values, even if relevance and trust in the source are low), and others staunchly refuse to believe the facts when the information comes from a source they don't explicitly trust.

Let's see if we can apply this to a number of possible scenarios:

The revolutions in Tunisia and Egypt

These events were highly dependent on message propagation. In this case, most messages would be graded as high-relevance and high-immediacy, and some with high severity (e.g., information on troop movements or police crackdowns). However, in any fast-changing context like this, certainty is low and trust-worthiness of the source takes over for trustworthiness of the message. That is, a message from your aunt is more trustworthy than a message from a journalist. Rumors can flourish and spread, sometimes leading crowds of people in the wrong direction.

Thus, we can explain why every revolution needs a coherent leadership—in a time of chaos, messages from a leader can carry both certainty (as the leader surely has better information or can convincingly fake knowledge), as well as charismatic trust in the message source.

Paul Revere's ride

This is a prime example of high severity, high immediacy, high relevance, and high certainty all in one. Even if the source was not well-known, the message had reached critical mass instantly. Resonance was high, since people already believed that the British attack was imminent. It also helped that Paul Revere did not send out a tweet to the world, but rather visited a string of towns—reaching critical mass in a large number of separate, smaller venues that later united against the British Army.

A commercial for a new TV

This has low to medium relevance to most of its audience (with the exception of a few that are in process of choosing a new TV the day it airs), low severity, low immediacy. To overcome this, advertisers must design messages that hit with high certainty ("this WILL improve your life"), trust for the source ("5 out of 6 doctors recommend…"), and high entertainment value. Other tactics might be more appropriate for used-car salesmen, amping up severity and immediacy ("Act NOW or this deal will disappear forever").

Resonance for commercials can be quite low, as many people are indifferent to brand names. Of course, in this case the exceptions dominate the rule. Apple spent years and billions of dollars to cultivate a base of fans, as do most sports teams and a number of other companies. Those that are successful in catering to the fan base are able to reap rewards even with mediocre messages—as long as these messages reinforce the existing ideas of the fans (we will discuss this in more detail in "A Simple Dynamic Model in Python" on page 121).

In the end, most commercials are quietly ignored—but once in a while, one goes viral and starts spreading on the Internet outside of the advertiser's campaign. Usually, this means that the commercial has a high entertainment value and is worth spending time on (see cost/benefit analysis above) on its own merits even when it triggers none of the other factors.

A chain letter

The chain letter is a curious member of this family. The message originates from somebody you know and trust in other matters. It originally draws you in with the entertainment value of a good story, but finishes with a severe and immediate consequence if you do not forward the letter. In this case, the certainty of harm is low,[4] but the cost of forwarding the email is low as well (and what if the letter is true?)

A LOLCat

I'm at a loss for words. Personally, I don't find them worthy of the download time, but I guess I am an atypical consumer of Internet media. For some, the entertainment value of a LOLCat is high enough not only to look at them or spread them, but also to create new ones. I can has extra time on my hands? [5]

Many other messages spread in the exact same way—think about religious messages and compare the message of the Catholic Church to that of a fire-and-brimstone preacher. While the message may be similar in content, the messages hit completely different notes. Or deconstruct an evening's worth of commercials, or the latest viral craze.

How Does Information Shape Networks (and Vice Versa)?

Information, ideas and views can change relatively rapidly, and in doing so, shape network structures. At the same time, the shape of networks controls where information can spread. As a result, we have a double feedback loop where social structure influences information transmission, and information influences change in social structure. In this section, we'll talk about the processes that make this happen—and attempt to build a simple dynamic model of information diffusion.

---

4. Even my aunt knows that, and still forwards 2-3 letters a week.

5. I did participate in the "All your base" craze in 2000. It was funnier then, I swear! A testament to immediacy, actually.

Birds of a Feather?

In "Theory of 2-Mode Networks" on page 96, we briefly mentioned the notion of homophily—creation of links between nodes as a function of how similar they are. While the idea has been apocryphal for hundreds of years (as a proverb "Birds of a feather flock together"), scientifically it was first addressed by Lazarsfeld and Merton in 1954.[6] They distinguished two types: *status homophily* and *value homophily*.

Status homophily means that individuals of a similar social class, wealth, and status are more likely to associate with each other than by chance. Value homophily means a tendency to associate with others who think in similar ways or like similar things, regardless of class and status.

American culture, of course, has been significantly more amenable to value homophily than many other societies where one's upbringing and membership of a class often clearly and unambiguously defines what kinds of information or cultural artifacts one may be exposed to. This is even more evident online, where "nobody knows you are a dog." One's online identity, while now pervasive and nearly permanent, is infinitely more malleable than an offline identity.

One of the differences between status homophily and value homophily is precisely this malleability. Social status and class can be considered permanent attributes—social mobility is generally too slow of a process to be captured in a social network study. Value homophily, on the other hand, runs "at Internet speed."

Homophily vs. Curiosity

Sociologists observed another interesting phenomenon—while homophily remains a strong social force, a second force can be in play if the two people are not very similar but not so different as to limit their ability to find topics for conversation. This force is curiosity or information seeking, and as a result, likelihood of connection takes a funny 2-hump shape as seen in Figure 6-3. The height and location of the "curiosity hill" is different for every person and is related to our novelty-seeking or novelty avoidance tendencies (in fact, it may be a part of our genetic makeup, specifically the number of D1 dopamine receptors in our brain)—but it always exists in some shape.

6. Lazarsfeld, P., and R.K. Merton. "Friendship as a Social Process: A Substantive and Methodological Analysis." In Freedom and Control in Modern Society, eds. Morroe Berger, Theodore Abel, and Charles H. Page. New York: Van Nostrand, 1954.

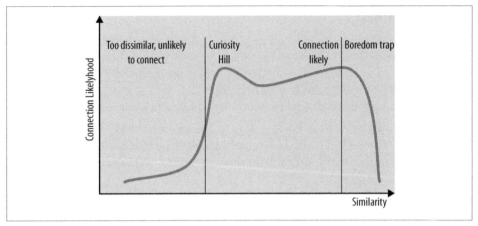

Figure 6-3. Homophily and curiosity

The final feature is the "boredom trap." Meeting a person who is exactly the same as you in every aspect provides no new information or stimulation—thus, the likelihood of connection drops off dramatically. The location and severity of the boredom trap also differs from person to person and also appears to be related to the way our brain processes and needs novelty.

The extremes of this spectrum are pathological—from autism, which is characterized with inability to process novelty and difficulty forming social ties and understanding others; to Williams syndrome, where novelty-seeking and gregariousness are taken to the extreme (and abstract and spatial reasoning is deficient).

You can also view this as a progression in time. Imagine a young couple that have just met. They might share some traits (both are young and good looking, if nothing else), but overall their level of homophily might be quite low; instead, their curiosity is at its peak. As the relationship progresses, they learn more about each other, even things they would rather not communicate. Eventually, the boy learns about his girlfriend's crippling student loans, and the girl learns about her boyfriend's nasty habit of leaving dirty socks everywhere. This is probably the bottom of a trough between curiosity and true homophily. If their relationship survives past that point, they will grow comfortable knowing nearly everything about each other and (hopefully) reach a ripe old age happily married. Except in the last 10 years or so, they will hardly speak a word to each other...why speak if you have nothing new to say?

Boundary Spanners

The fact that all of us have different genetic makeups and personalities contributes to the fact that our social networks are by far not uniform, and homophily is by far not universal. Some individuals are comfortable in the position of *boundary spanners*, where they maintain connections to multiple groups that exhibit very low homophily. Not only they serve as a crucial conduit for information, they also can take advantage of opportunities of brokerage and arbitrage—whether it means establishing trade between tribes in the Stone Age or working on Wall Street. We have already discussed this in "The "Forbidden Triad" and Structural Holes" on page 72—but boundary spanning can be also seen through the lens of information diffusion.

Weak Ties

In the 1970s, Mark Granovetter conducted a study of blue-collar workers in a certain neighborhood of South Boston. Most of his respondents were Irish immigrants, worked in construction or other skilled-labor trades, and spent a considerable amount of time in the pubs. Jobs, especially construction jobs, were fairly unstable, and at any given time a good proportion of the population was unemployed and looking for work. The goal of the project was to learn how information about jobs moves through the social networks.

The local pub was the social hub—everyone had a regular hangout and knew most of the other men that went to the pub. So, the original goal was to find out the role of pub conversations in someone's ability to find a new job.

However, the result was rather surprising—people found out about new jobs through their regular pub friends only ~30% of the time. Most of the time, information about jobs came from distant connections—a cousin, friend's in-laws, etc. (that is, people with whom only a weak network link exists).

Granovetter theorized that strong links increase the homophily—so when one needs novel information (e.g., when looking for a job), the people connected to ego with strong ties are less likely to possess any new data. At the same time, people connected by a weak tie can be in a completely different place (in terms of access to information).

Dunbar Number and Weak Ties

In his paper (which has now become a classic),[7] Robin Dunbar shows that the average size of a human social network (i.e., an average degree centrality) is 150—and that this number is cognitively limited by the size of our prefrontal cortex, or our innate ability to reason about other people and relationships.

However, it's not quite as simple. I'd like to show the dissection of the Dunbar number as a pyramid (see Figure 6-4). At the top, our strongest ties are our immediate family and best friends, people we interact with on a daily basis and consider close and trustworthy. Dunbar measured the size of this immediate group as 7 on average—it includes our spouse, parents, siblings, and children. Note that this is the same number as the estimated size of a human working memory (7 +/- 3), so we can surmise that our immediate and closest social connections are those that we can or must keep in our working memory.

7. Hill, R. A., and Dunbar, R. I. M. "Social network size in humans". *Human Nature* 14 (2003).

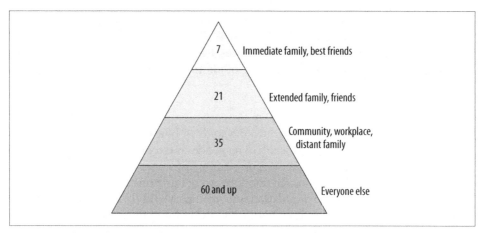

Figure 6-4. The Dunbar pyramid

The list is stratified further into the "extended family" (including a group of friends, cousins, in-laws, etc.): people that you do not necessarily interact with on a daily basis or consider the closest. The next stratum, a "tribe," includes coworkers, a larger circle of friends and acquaintances, and distant family members. The final stratum catches everyone else, essentially your weak ties.

But where are your Facebook friends and Twitter followers? Most likely, at the very bottom of the pyramid. As you can see from the description of the relationships above, as we go down the pyramid, the emotional and information-sharing content of the relationship go down as the quantity goes up. So, how much emotional attention does your Twitter follower number 837 get? Not much at all.

For a company in business of serving customers, personal engagement in social media is paramount for precisely this reason. When a company representative engages with a Twitter follower on a personal level (e.g., responding to a complaint), he or she invests some emotional energy into the relationship. Since the exchange happens in public, it bolsters not only the relationship with an existing customer, but also a perceived potential for a relationship for other Twitter followers.

Since every person has different preferences for close and personal contact, the pyramid may take very different forms for everyone. The authors personally know several people whose majority of social engagement comes from Facebook and blogs; essentially merging their online following and their extended family ranks. Because maintaining an online following requires less emotional investment per follower, their degree centrality can reach thousands while their immediate family seldom sees them at all. One such person, a cyber-nomad, has gone as far as be technically homeless for several years, living on people's couches and circumnavigating the country several times a year.

A Simple Dynamic Model in Python

Now that we had our fill of theory and examples, let us try to model information diffusion in a social network. We will build a very simple agent-based model in which agents can influence each other and reach a consensus (if such is possible) within their social network.

This model was originally proposed by Noah Friedkin in 1998.[8] The model follows a very simple premise: everyone comes into a discussion with their own take on the problem (or their own attitude), and everybody accepts influence from their friends in the network, to a degree. Let us also make an assumption that the information that our agents will be exchanging is about a single real number between 0 and 1. This could mean the likelihood of the stock market going up, or possibly the likelihood of an agent trying an illegal drug (this model has been used to study spread of information in both of these contexts)

Let us then set our simple model. We are not going to use an agent-based modeling toolkit, or a simulation toolkit—but we don't really need them to build this model.

Let us start by defining a Python class for a person:

```
class Person(object):

    def __init__(self, id):
        #Start with a single initial preference
        self.id=id
        self.i = r.random()
        self.a = self.i
        #we value initial opinion and subsequent information equally
        self.alpha=0.8

    def __str__(self):
        return(str(self.id))
```

A *Person* has an ID, and 3 important numbers: `self.i` is an initial attitude, `self.a` is an acquired attitude (it accumulates all input from *Person*'s friends), and finally, `self.alpha` is what I would call "the gullibility factor" (i.e., the higher `alpha` is, the more likely I am to trust my friends' opinions and distrust my initial knowledge). For the sake of the initial approach, let us assume that everyone is gullible to exactly the same degree.

Now, let's create a network of *Person* nodes. NetworkX allows one to use any object as a graph node, and we'll use this feature:

---

8. Friedkin, N.E. *A Structural Theory of Social Influence*. Cambridge University Press, 1998.

```
density=0.9
g=net.Graph()

## create a network of Person objects
for i in range(10):
    p=Person(i)
    g.add_node(p)

##this will be a simple random graph, every pair of nodes has an
##equal probability of connection
for x in g.nodes():
    for y in g.nodes():
        if r.random()<=density: g.add_edge(x,y)

## draw the resulting graph and color the nodes by their value
col=[n.a for n in g.nodes()]
pos=net.spring_layout(g)
net.draw_networkx(g,pos=pos, node_color=col)
```

First, we initialize an empty graph and add 10 objects of type *Person* to the graph. Then, we iterate through every possible combination of 2 nodes. With probability equal to the *density* parameter, we shall add an edge between 2 nodes. This kind of graph generation is called an Erdos-Renyi algorithm;[9] it is the simplest way to generate a random graph, and results in a normally distributed degree centrality.

Erdos-Renyi random graphs have been used as a benchmark for many graph-based algorithms and models, but now we know that they are quite unrealistic as a representation of a social network, because most social networks have a long-tail distribution of degrees (e.g., power-law). However, since other methods for generating networks are significantly more complex, and beyond the scope of this model, we'll use the simplest tool out there. The network should look similar to Figure 6-5.

Now the preliminaries are set up, let's create the simulation itself. Insert the following function into the Person class:

```
def step(self):
    #loop through the neighbors and aggregate their preferences
    neighbors=g[self]
    #all nodes in the list of neighbors are equally weighted, including self
    w=1/float((len(neighbors)+1))
    s=w*self.a
    for node in neighbors:
        s+=w*node.a

    # update my beliefs = initial belief plus sum of all influences
    self.a=(1-self.alpha)*self.i + self.alpha*s
```

---

9. Erdos, P. and A. Rényi. "On Random Graphs I" in *Publ. Math. Debrecen* 6 (1959), 290–297

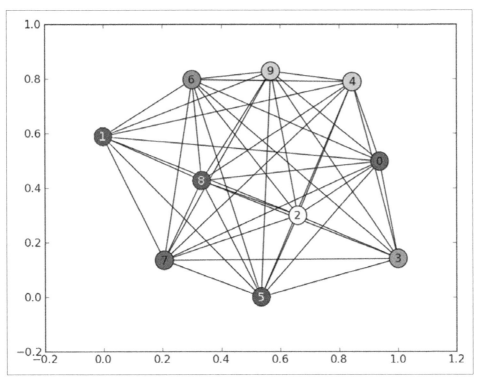

Figure 6-5. Network of agents for diffusion model

This function updates a Person's attitude (*a*) based on a weighted sum of her friends' attitudes, and the person's gullibility factor *alpha*. First, we shall compute the weights. For the sake of simplicity, everyone's opinion is weighted equally (line 5).

Then, we compute a weighted sum of the Person's own opinion, and everyone else's opinions (lines 6-8). Finally, we update the current opinion (line 11) by saying that a Person's opinion at time *t* equals the objective knowledge multiplied by gullibility factor, added to the weighted sum of her friends' opinions.

Finally, let us run this in a loop to see how the network changes over time:

```
## repeat for 30 time periods
for i in range(30):
    ## iterate through all nodes in the network and tell them to make a step
    for node in g.nodes():
        node.step()

    ## collect new attitude data, print it to the terminal and plot it.
    col=[n.a for n in g.nodes()]
    print col
    plot.plot(col)
```

The result of running the model for 30 time periods would look somewhat like Figure 6-6. Over time, the agents become closer and closer to each other in their opinions, although they never quite achieve total consensus.

Let us now play with the parameters a little bit. What if all agents were perfectly gullible and accepted everything their friends said? Let's set *alpha = 1.0* and see. Figure 6-7 shows that everyone reaches consensus quickly—even if this consensus is completely wrong given the facts.

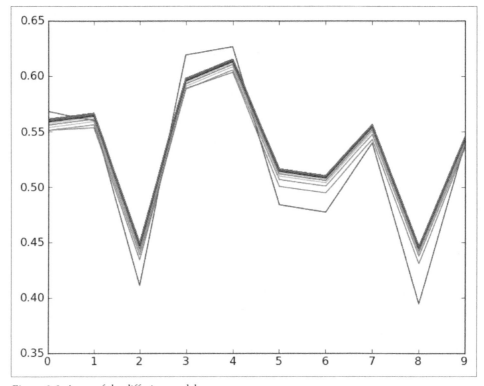

Figure 6-6. A run of the diffusion model

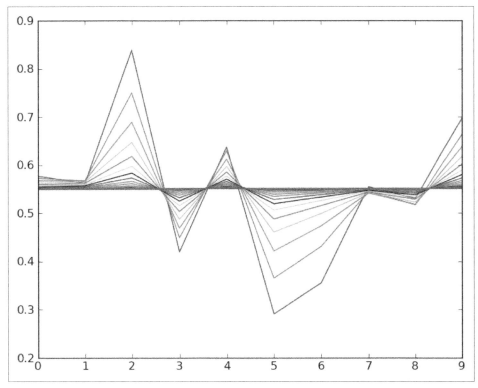

Figure 6-7. Consensus in the diffusion model

Influencers in the Midst

Now let's suppose that several propaganda agents (influencers, evangelists) are inserted in the midst of the network. Each of these influences has an immovable extreme position In the case of this model, this attitude = 1 while all others fall elsewhere on the 0 to 1 spectrum.

We define an influencer as a special kind of a person in the model:

```
class Influencer(Person):
    def __init__(self,id):
        self.id=id
        self.i = r.random()
        self.a = 1 ## opinion is strong and immovable

    def step(self):
        pass
```

Then, we add several of the influencers to the network and connect them to the other agents:

```
influencers=2
connections=4
##add the influencers to the network and connect each to 3 other nodes
for i in range(influencers):
    inf=Influencer("Inf"+str(i))
    for x in range(connections):
        g.add_edge(r.choice(g.nodes()), inf)
```

Then, run the model as usual:

```
## repeat for 30 time periods
for i in range(30):
    ## iterate through all nodes in the network and tell them to make a step
    for node in g.nodes():
        node.step()

    ## collect new attitude data, print it to the terminal and plot it.
    col=[n.a for n in g.nodes()]
    print col
    plot.plot(col)
```

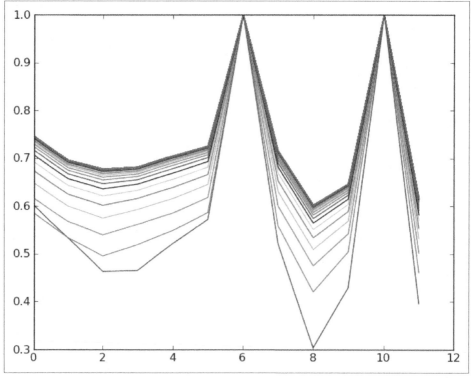

Figure 6-8. Adding two influencers to the network accelerates movement towards an extreme value

Figure 6-8 shows that the 2 influencers have a strong effect—however, initial positions still do not allow the agents to fully migrate to the extreme positions. The more influencers are present, the more likely is the motion toward a consensus on an extreme value.

This model is highly simplified, and does not take into account many of the factors that go into diffusion of information. There is no homophily, there are no critical mass effects, and the progress is very linear. However, it's a start. We'll continue building this up as we go along.

Exercises for the Reader

The model implementation I have presented here is oversimplified to the extreme. The reader is well-advised to try the following ideas:

- Make the gullibility factor heterogenous rather than set for the entire group of agents.
- Experiment with scale-free networks using a variety of parameters instead of using simple random networks.
- Implement trust weighting for friends' opinions (i.e., not weighting all opinions equally, but rather based on strength of a tie between actors).
- Make calculation of attitudes multidimensional—a real person has many attitudes toward different things, and so should the agents.

Coevolution of Networks and Information

Now we will modify the model of influence so that networks allow for change in the network as well as the attitudes of individuals and information content of the network. First, let us remove the step function from the previous model, and instead introduce an interaction function that exchanges information with one agent, and not with the entire set of neighbors. The same idea of the gullibility ratio applies here as well:

```
## instead of looking at all of the neighbors,
##let's pick a random node and exchange information with him
## this will create an edge and weigh it with their similarity.
def interact(self):
    partner=r.choice(g.nodes())
    s=0.5*(self.a + partner.a)
    # update my beliefs = initial belief plus sum of all influences
    self.a=(1-self.alpha)*self.i + self.alpha*s
    g.add_edge(self,partner,weight=(1-self.a-partner.a))
```

So far, this is random choice. After the interaction and reception of information, we will create an edge between the two nodes. This edge will be weighted by similarity—the more similar the nodes become, the stronger their connection.

However, we also know that connections decay after a certain period of time. The easiest way to describe it is with a constant decay rate:

```
v(t+1)=v(t)*(1-decay_rate)
```

The decay rate in real-world networks is quite low, while in online networks can be significantly higher (as it is easier to "defriend" someone on Facebook or simply tune out their messages than it is to have an argument with a real-world friend). However, this model is pretty abstract, so we'll choose an easy number. Let's say that network links decay 1% per time period.

 A time period in this simulation is entirely arbitrary. However, one could reasonably link it (as well as the decay rate) to the notion of strength of ties as a function of communication frequency, as described in "What Is a Graph?" on page 19.

So, let us initialize the network in the same manner as we did before and run the simulation. Figure 6-9 shows how a well-connected node builds a small group of similar followers around him, while the less well-connected nodes remain with contrary opinions. Thus, nodes with widely varying opinions can coexist peacefully and multiple consensus points can emerge (Figure 6-10).

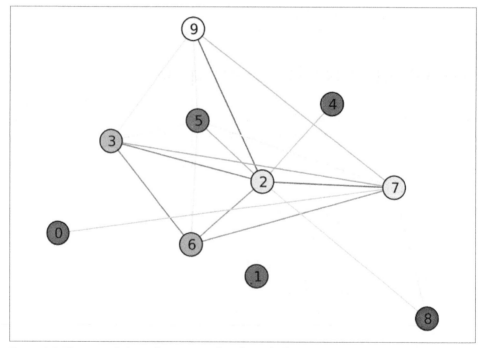

Figure 6-9. The network shows that a group of similar nodes becomes better connected while dissimilar nodes are on the periphery

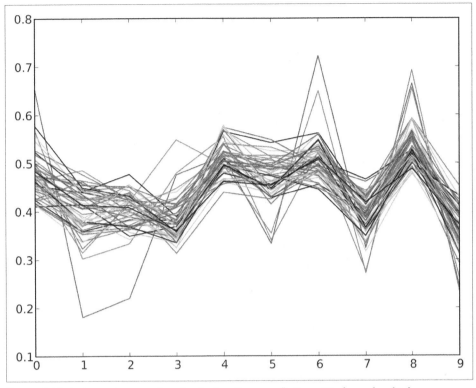

Figure 6-10. A change in network and attitudes allows conflicting attitudes and multiple consensuses to coexist

However, this still relies on the notion of random choice of communication partners —which, we know, is not true (see "How Does Information Shape Networks (and Vice Versa)?" on page 116). So, now let us implement a notion of homophily. To do so, each *Person* will maintain a list of people that he knows, and some idea of how similar he is to them. In this case, we already store the homophily value in the edge of the graph, in the following line:

```
g.add_edge(self,partner,weight=(1-self.a-partner.a))
```

But before we start utilizing this information to pick partners, let us talk a little bit about choice. As we discussed in "How Does Information Shape Networks (and Vice Versa)?" on page 116, we have a higher probability of choosing someone we are similar with—but a secondary peak in interest lets us talk to people that are very different. Some communication may be random as well. To allow us to pick partners with a probability proportional to their similarity (or dissimilarity), we implement a procedure called a "roulette choice."

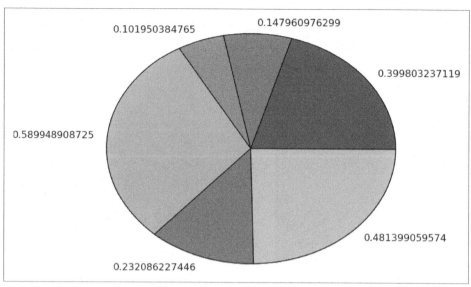

0.147960976299

0.101950384765

0.399803237119

0.589948908725

0.481399059574

0.232086227446

Figure 6-11. The weighted roulette for choosing network partners

Imagine that a roulette wheel exists with unequally weighted sectors (Figure 6-11). Thus, betting on the some sectors has a greater probability of winning, despite the roulette spin being fair (i.e., uniformly distributed). We implement the roulette method by constructing a list of communication partners, and repeating their names as many times as needed, proportional to their similarity. Then, a uniform random selection from the list will return us an appropriately weighted roulette selection:

```
def _roulette_choice(self,names,values, inverse=False):
    """
    roulette method makes unequally weighted choices based on a set of values
    Names and values should be lists of equal lengths
    values are between 0 and 1
    if inverse=False, names with higher values have a higher probability of choice;
    if inverse=True, names with lower values have hight probability

    """
    wheel=names
    for i in range(len(names)):
        if not inverse:
            wheel.extend([names[i] for x in range(1+int(values[i]*10))])
        else:
            wheel.extend([names[i] for x in range(1+int((1-values[i])*10))])
    return(r.choice(wheel))
```

Finally, we need to modify the `interact()` method to allow for use of the roulette method. We roll the dice one more time, and decide if the communication partner will be similar (with a probability of 0.6), dissimilar (with a probability of 0.3) or entirely random (with probability of 0.1). If someone has nobody to talk to, he will pick randomly and try to establish some ties:

```
def interact(self):
    """
    instead of looking at all of the neighbors,
    let's pick a random node and exchange information with him
    this will create an edge and weigh it with their similarity.

    Phase II -- make roulette choice instead of random choice
    """
    neighbors=g[self].keys()
    values=[v['weight'] for v in g[self].values()]

    ## roll dice and decide to communicate with
    ## similar (0.6), dissimilar(0.3) or random (0.1)
    roll=r.random()
    if r <= 0.1 or len(neighbors)==0:
        partner=r.choice(g.nodes())
    elif r<=0.4:
        partner=self._roulette_choice(neighbors,values,inverse=True)
    else:
        partner=self._roulette_choice(neighbors,values,inverse=False)

    w=0.5
    s=self.a*w + partner.a*w
    # update my beliefs = initial belief plus sum of all influences
    self.a=(1-self.alpha)*self.i + self.alpha*s
    g.add_edge(self,partner,weight=(1-self.a-partner.a))
```

Let us also modify the model to output a few more plots. The first one will be a "consensus plot"—displaying the mean opinion of everyone in the network, and the minimum and maximum values:

```
def consensus(g):
    """
    Calculcate consensus opinion of the graph
    """
    aa=[n.a for n in g.nodes()]
    return min(aa),max(aa),sum(aa)/len(aa)
```

On every iteration of the model, we'll append the consensus values for the network to a list, and plot the result at the end:

```
cons=[]
for i in range(runtime):
    for node in g.nodes():
        node.interact()
....
....simulation code is here....
....
    cons.append(consensus(g))
....
....after the end of the run....
....
plot.figure(i+1)
plot.plot(cons)
```

Also, let us explore the values of the edges by plotting their histogram:

```
plot.figure(i+2)
plot.hist([e['weight'] for f,t,e in g.edges(data=True)])
```

 The complete code of the model can be downloaded from GitHub (*https://github.com/maksim2042/SNABook/chapter6*).

Let us now reload the model and run it. A sample result is shown in Figures 6-12 and 6-13.

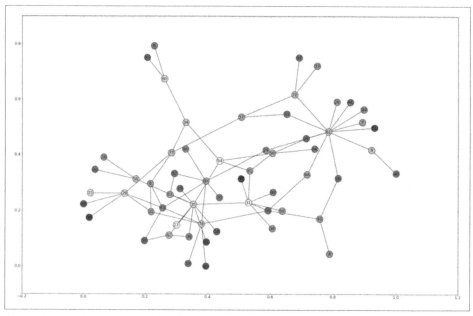

Figure 6-12. In the final network, nodes can be quite dissimilar in their opinions

Our first observation is that the network quickly approaches a stable state—but this stable state is not a consensus, but rather, a wide swath of acceptable opinions that excludes both high and low extremes, and encourages a comfortable average. In the absence of opinion leaders, the exact place where this average lands is fairly random—but we can be quite sure that, if our random number generator is fair, it will not be anywhere near an extreme.

The network does not become homogenized in clusters—rather, nodes with opinions within acceptable range coexist in a stable dynamic equilibrium. How is this possible?

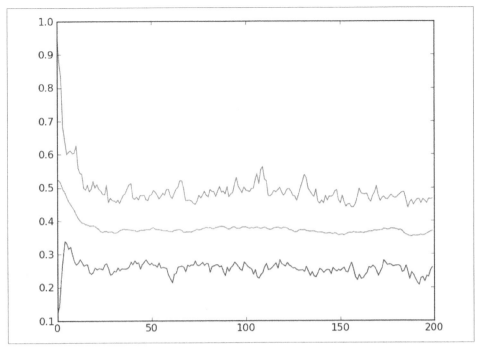

Figure 6-13. The network converges to a range of acceptable opinions, but allows quite a bit of diversity within it

We discussed this exact mechanism in this chapter—it's weak ties. If one plots a histogram of tie strength in the network (Figure 6-14), one will discover that strong edges are rare (as well as exceptionally weak ones). Instead, edge strength seems to be distributed around a mean of ~0.3: a good, solid weak tie.

This further reinforces the Dunbar pyramid of tie strength—strong ties are rare and require full consensus (which is also rare), while weak ties are easier to establish and maintain.

Exercises for the Reader

- Add back the influencers. How do they change the dynamic? If several influencers are in conflict (have diametrically opposing views), will the network split?
- Add shocks to the model. For example, an agent could, at a random moment, change his opinion to an extreme value. Will his friends "talk sense into him"?
- Add agents with different communication capabilities; for example, broadcasters who can talk to everyone at once.
- Build a model of an election based upon this model. Several candidates vie for attention of the population. How should they campaign to affect the outcome?

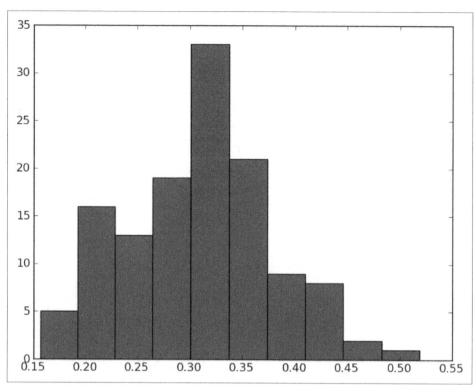

Figure 6-14. Most ties are weak and medium-weak ties, just as the Dunbar pyramid shows

Why Model Networks?

In this section, we have demonstrated that, with a few lines of code, we can encapsulate theories of network dynamics and change, and attempt to validate them by running simulations. Frequently, in an environment where one deals with a lot of empirical data, it is difficult to formulate a succinct theory of what makes the network change, and what is the direction of change. Models force the simplicity of theory, and allow one to test multiple ideas quickly.[10]

This model can serve as a test base for other models of information diffusion. For example, imagine a network where certain nodes blink in and out of existence, bringing with them some unique information. Or, a network that is allowed to evolve undisturbed for a while, and then is "attacked" with novel information (e.g., the "missionaries and savages" problem). Alternatively, imagine this as a base for a model of a drug trafficking ring, and place a network analyst in the seat of a police officer who wants to disrupt the flow of information through the network. The possibilities are nearly endless.

10. The models in this chapter took Max less than 4 hours to program and test.

The entire field of Computational Social Science (CSS) has risen from a merger of Social Network Analysis, Artificial Life, Artificial Intelligence, and a number of other fields. But this, perhaps, is a topic for our next book.

## CHAPTER 7

Graph Data in the Real World

So far we have been dealing with fairly simple datasets, in flat files. Flat files are great for quick analysis: they are portable and mostly human-readable, not to mention accessible to UNIX powertools. This convenience, however, fades quickly when our involvement with the data broadens, as we show in Figure 7-1.

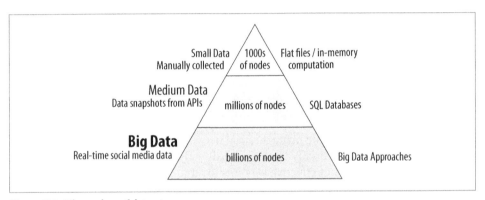

Figure 7-1. The realms of data sizes

NetworkX is a spectacular tool, with one important limitation: memory. The graph we want to study has to fit *entirely* in memory. To put this in perspective, a mostly connected graph of 1,000 nodes (binomial, connection probability 0.8 = 800,000 edges) uses 100MB of memory, without any attributes. The same graph with 2,000 nodes (and almost 2 million edges) uses 500MB. In general, memory usage is bounded by $O(n)=n+n^2=n(n+1)$. One can easily find this out firsthand by creating a graph in an interactive Python session and observing its memory usage.

Until the late 1990s, social network data has been gathered and compiled manually. The ways to gather data included surveys, psychology experiments, and working with large amounts of text ("text coding") to extract nodes and relationships. As a result, gathering a dataset of a few hundred nodes was considered a monumental effort worthy of a Ph.D.; there was simply no need to handle larger datasets.

Now, suppose we were scientifically curious about what goes on on Twitter. Twitter offers a free sample stream of roughly 1% of their entire traffic. At the time of writing, the sample stream carries over 1.2 million messages a day. Assuming an average tweet with all the attributes weighs around 1KB, the nodes alone are likely to take up 1.5GB. While the hard limits will depend on hardware and system configuration, it should be evident how quickly the in-memory graph database like NetworkX becomes unmanageable.

Medium Data: The Tradition

The traditional solution to process large and complex datasets has been the relational SQL-based databases. Not only does this extend the size boundary to lots and lots of cheap hard drive space versus scarce and expensive RAM, but it allows multiple components of the system to access the same data in one central place. Countless software systems and frameworks were designed over the years that back out to a SQL database. Whatever the environment the analyst finds herself in, chances are there is a SQL backend. This, of course, includes our personal favorite: Django.

It only makes sense to integrate manage social network data the same way we manage the rest of it: by storing and modifying the graph directly in the database. In this chapter, we demonstrate a simple but effective way to store and modify NetworkX graphs in a SQLite3 database.

Big Data: The Future, Starting Today

We must jump ahead and admit that the traditional solution is not without problems itself. Two important things happened in recent years: relentless progress has brought us massive social networking platforms along with massive data; and MapReduce systems have, in a rather timely way, reached maturity. The real "big data," the kind commonly available nowadays, is too big for relational databases (not that our tried-and-true RDBMSs are ultimately incapable of handling it, but the complexity of such a solution is very likely to cause fatal hair-pulling in a previously sane and happy person). It is with great joy the authors note that we have entered the age that favors the simple. Read more on this in "Social Networks and Big Data" on page 151.

"Small Data"—Flat File Representations

When we talk about "small data"—i.e., datasets that do not require the complexity of a relational database or a distributed solution, we frequently turn to flat files. In Social Network Analysis, there exist a variety of flat file formats, from a proprietary binary format, to a few useful text-based formats (each with its own limitations), to "enterprise-grade" XML formats. For a while, up until the early 2000s, it seemed like everybody (including yours truly) was inventing new ways to encode network data and promoting them as an "emerging standard."

The community has since settled into a collective *yawn* over data interchange. XML has proven to be too verbose (but still gets a lot of use when rich data is required), the number of text-based formats dwindled to one or two, and the binary formats are no longer used for interchange.

NetworkX came out of the door supporting a number of different formats; we'll take a quick overview of what you're likely to encounter "in the wild" and what to do with it.

EdgeList Files

Perhaps the simplest way to store graph data is the Edgelist format. Its main advantage —besides simplicity—is the ability to easily import and export files into Excel or other spreadsheets; however, this also means that the files are significantly less expressive then the more complex ones.

Edgelist files do not carry attribute data about nodes—but can carry arbitrary amounts of data concerning edges. The file format is exceedingly simple:

```
<from_id> <to_id> <data1> <data2> ... <dataN>
foo bar 1 2
```

where from_id and to_id are string name or ID of the nodes that specify a graph edge, and columns <data1>...<dataN> are an arbitrary list of values that are assigned to this edge. No column headings are supplied with this data, so it's up to the user to determine which column means what. To make things a bit more rigorous, freeform data can be kept in a Python dict format:

```
<from_id> <to_id> <dict>
foo bar {'weight':1,'color':'green' }
```

Edgelists are easy to generate from other data processing tools—e.g., as a product of an SQL query or a file read from the filesystem:

```
# read an edgelist from a file while disregarding any of the data
g=read_edgelist(<filename>)

#read an edgelist and import the freeform data column as a list of attributes
g=read_edgelist(<filename>,data=True)
```

```
# read an edgelist and use the first numerical value of the data
# as an edge weight.
g=read_valued_edgelist(<filename>)
```

.net Format

Not to be confused with the Microsoft .NET architecture, .net files represent a very simple (if somewhat limited) format for expressing network data using ASCII text. This format was first used by a tool called *Pajek*, and is now something like a lingua franca of network data interchange.

The files look something like this:

```
*Vertices 3
1 "Node1" 0.0 0.0 0.0 ic Green bc Brown
2 "Node2" 0.0 0.0 0.0 ic Green bc Brown
3 "Node3" 0.0 0.0 0.0 ic Green bc Brown
*Arcs
1 2 3 c Green
2 3 5 c Black
*Edges
1 3 4 c Green
```

The file is separated by sections, each section name starting with an asterisk (*):

Vertices

This section contains nodes' names and attributes. The header *Vertices* is immediately followed by the number of vertices expected. Pajek expects this number to be accurate, although it is entirely optional elsewhere.

Each of the lines contains the following columns:

- Numeric ID of the node (in sequence)
- Name of the node in quotes
- Node coordinates (x, y, z) and colors (background and foreground). These are non-zero only if the Pajek layout has been precomputed; they are optional for use in NetworkX

*Arcs and *Edges*

Arcs are directed edges, while Edges are undirected. If the graph is undirected, the Arcs section will not be present; if the graph is directed, the Edges section can be omitted. Each of the rows contains:

- from_id (a numeric ID of a node from the Vertices section)
- to_id (another numeric ID of a node)
- weight (value of the edge or arc)
- color (only if doing the layout in Pajek)

To read a Pajek-formatted file in NetworkX, use the following command:

```
g = net.read_pajek(<filename>)
```

The command returns a NetworkX graph object: a DiGraph if directed edges are present, and a Graph otherwise. To write a Pajek file, use this command:

```
net.write_pajek(<filename>)
```

GML, GraphML, and other XML Formats

GML (Graph Modeling Language) and GraphML are two distant-cousin XML-based formats. A variety of tools support one or both of them—ranging from software for analysis of protein interactions, to project planning and supply chain planning systems. GraphML is more expressive, as it allows for hierarchical graphs, multigraphs, and other special cases—but for purposes of the SNA, they are about equivalent.

A GraphML file looks something like this:

```
<?xml version="1.0" encoding="UTF-8"?>
<graphml>
  <key id="d0" for="node" attr.name="color" attr.type="string">yellow</key>
  <key id="d1" for="edge" attr.name="weight" attr.type="double"/>
  <graph id="G" edgedefault="undirected">
    <node id="n0">
      <data key="d0">green</data>
    </node>
    <node id="n1"/>
    <node id="n2">
      <data key="d0">blue</data>
    </node>
    <node id="n3">
      <data key="d0">red</data>
    </node>

.... more node definitions....

    <edge id="e0" source="n0" target="n2">
      <data key="d1">1.0</data>
    </edge>
    <edge id="e1" source="n0" target="n1">
      <data key="d1">1.0</data>
    </edge>
    <edge id="e2" source="n1" target="n3"/>

.... more edges ....
  </graph>
</graphml>
```

As you can see, it takes 23 lines of XML (not counting comments) to describe a graph with 4 nodes and 3 edges. Much of the text in the file contains XML tags; this leads to XML files being much larger then plain-text representations.

In 2003, I designed another XML-based format called DyNetML. It is currently supported by ORA (Organizational Risk Analyzer), AutoMap (Network Text Analysis software), and a number of other tools from the CASOS lab at Carnegie Mellon (*http://www.casos.cs.cmu.edu*). However, DyNetML was not widely adopted by any other organizations, so it remains in use only within its own ecosystem.

In general, XML-based graphs are much more expressive and flexible than any of the text-file based formats. However, we pay for it with increased file size and long parsing times.

Ancient Binary Format—##h Files

UCINET, a commercial Windows-based tool for SNA, has been considered "the Excel of SNA" for almost 20 years. It is a GUI-driven system encompassing hundreds of different modules, and is arguably the most comprehensive SNA tool on the planet. It is used in almost every SNA course, and taught to sociology and public policy students.

Unfortunately, the system was developed in Turbo Pascal in the 90s and the programmer who built its file I/O has long since vanished. As a result, we have a difficult-to-use proprietary file format that cannot keep up with the modern file systems, and cannot be reverse-engineered.

If you download UCINET's demo, it will come with a set of data files—probably the most likely place you will encounter files of this type.

Each dataset (network or a list of nodes or a table) requires 2 files. Both files have the same filename; the first file has an extension *h*, and the second *d*.

As far as using these files in NetworkX, you will likely have to download UCINET and convert them using the Export function, to a *.net* format.

"Medium Data": Database Representation

Previously, we showed you how to read and write Pajek files with NetworkX (""Small Data"—Flat File Representations" on page 139). Using the same idea, we will now demonstrate how do the same with a SQL-backed representation. Not only that, we will be able to add, remove, and modify nodes and edges in the stored graph directly in the database, without having to load the graph to memory.

For this example we'll use SQLite3 (*http://www.sqlite.org/*), a tiny but powerful zero-conf embedded SQL database engine. Upgrading to a "real" SQL database server is nothing more than a simple drop-in replacement; the code and the queries remain the same.

This implementation is simplified for educational purposes, not exactly industrially optimized production code. However, it does provide a good starting point for a useable implementation.

Seeing that a graph is nothing more than a collection of nodes and node pairs, we start with a simple schema (Figure 7-2):

```
def _prepare_tables(conn, name):
    c = conn.cursor()
    c.execute('drop table if exists "%s_edges"' % name)
    c.execute('drop table if exists "%s_nodes"' % name)
    c.execute('create table "%s_nodes" (node, attributes)' % name)
    c.execute('create table "%s_edges" (efrom, eto, attributes)' % name)
    conn.commit()
    c.close()
```

This function takes a SQLite (or compatible) connection (in this case, nothing more than an extended file pointer) and a graph name. In SQLite, unspecified types default to "string".

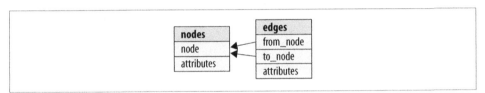

Figure 7-2. Database schema for storing network data

What are Cursors?

Cursors are special database objects used to traverse tables. Considering that communication with the database server usually happens over a network, it is rarely desirable to return all of the results at once—that would put unnecessary strain on the server and the network, not to mention client-side memory. When a cursor executes a query, it returns another special object called a *result set*: a pointer into a set of results not yet returned by the server. The client then iterates over the result set, asking for one or several rows at a time, and the server only has to fetch them in small batches. This is partial *lazy evaluation*.

What are Transactions?

Transactions are a safety feature that help prevent query errors from leaving data in a corrupt state, by executing a batch of operations *atomically*. Once a transaction is started, no changes are made to the actual data. It can then be either *committed* if no errors have occurred; or otherwise, *rolled back*. Committing a transaction commits the changes to the database, while a rollback discards them.

 A leading underscore in the function name indicates the function is not meant to be called from outside the module (a soft "private"). A double underscore signals something *really* private. This is supported by a common convention (and by some smart editors), but not directly enforced by the language. We, Pythonistas, are a disciplined bunch.

Names

Aside from nodes and edges, NetworkX graphs have one more important piece of data: a name. In a database we can store multiple objects, so let's assume that a name uniquely identifies a graph. For simplicity, we'll use the graph name as part of the table name.

 Professional drivers on a closed course. Do not attempt. The practice of string substitutions in SQL queries is *NOT SAFE*. We only do it here for the sake of simplicity. Also, the code is small enough that *we know* we have total control over the name parameter and it will not be used for malice. But you, in the real world, will not. So please don't.

To avoid the problem of spaces and other irregularities, let us convert the name to a nice mush of alphanumeric characters with Base64: [1]

```
def _encode(name):
    ''' Before using graph names in tables we need to convert
    to something that won't upset sqlite.'''
    return base64.encodestring(name).replace('\n', '')

def _decode(name):
    return base64.decodestring(name)

>>> _encode("O HAI, I am a long string with punctuation and spaces!")
'TyBIQUksIEkgYWOgYSBsb25nIHNOcmluZyB3aXRoIHB1bmNOdWF0aW9uIGFuZCBzcGFjZXMh'

>>>
_decode('TyBIQUksIEkgYWOgYSBsb25nIHNOcmluZyB3aXRoIHB1bmNOdWF0aW9uIGFuZCBzcGFjZXMh')
'O HAI, I am a long string with punctuation and spaces!'
```

---

1. Base64 is an encoding that represents binary data in ASCII printable format. Here we use it for its side effect of eradicating spaces.

No problem.

Nodes as Data, Attributes as ?

In NetworkX a node is an object—it can be anything. Similarly, node/edge attributes are dictionaries of objects. Here we restrict nodes to primitive types (integers and strings) and attribute objects to "simple" types (those that have JSON representation —this rules out some complex objects, but not all!). We use JSON to *serialize* objects.[2]

 JSON (*http://www.json.org/*) is a simple plain text data interchange format; we think of it as a sane replacement to XML. In Python, JSON conversion functionality is provided by `simplejson`.

The Class

We want to operate on our stored graph, and for that we need to know a few things, such as the table names and the location of the database. What we need is a class:

```
class SqlGraph(object):
    def __init__(self, sqlfile, name):
        self.conn = sqlite3.connect(sqlfile)
        self.name = _encode(name)

    def add_node(self, node, attr_dict=None):
        cursor = self.conn.cursor()
        attributes = simplejson.dumps(attr_dict)
        cursor.execute('''insert or replace into "%s_nodes" (node, attributes)
            values(?,?)''' % self.name, (node, attributes))
        self.conn.commit()
        cursor.close()
```

To add a node we simply store it and its JSONified attributes as two strings in the appropriate table.

Notice anything wrong with that function? If that looks like too much work for a simple insert query—it is. Creating cursors and committing transactions are considered "expensive" operations—they can take significantly more time than an `cursor.execute()` call. If we were to call `add_node()` in a loop, there could be a noticeable performance penalty. This penalty is unnecessary and avoidable. So let's rewrite the code:

```
    def add_node(self, node, attr_dict=None, cursor=None):
        _cursor = cursor or self.conn.cursor()
        attributes = simplejson.dumps(attr_dict)
        _cursor.execute('''insert or replace into "%s_nodes" (node, attributes)
            values(?,?)''' % self.name, (node, attributes))
        self.conn.commit()
```

2. (De)serialization is a technique of reversibly converting an object into a static format (byte array or text string) for transmission or storage.

```
    if cursor:
        cursor.close()
...
    cursor = connection.cursor()
    for node in nodes:
        graph.add_node(node, cursor=cursor)
    connection.commit()
    cursor.close()
```

Ah, much better. Now we can create a cursor and commit only once, regardless of how many nodes are added. You may notice a few new Python tricks:

Short-circuit evaluation

x = a or b is exactly the same as:

```
if a:
    x = a
else:
    x = b
```

It is important to note that when a is true, then b is never evaluated (or called if b is a function call)—guaranteed. The evaluation stops the moment the resulting boolean expression is known, hence the term.

Keyword arguments and default values

Declaring function arguments in the form *name=value* provides a default value (in this case, None) and makes that argument a keyword argument. When argument names coincide with variables, this may be confusing. In add_node(node, cursor=cursor), the first literal "cursor" is the name of the argument, and the second is the cursor variable that was just defined.

Functions and Decorators

Before we proceed to methods that delete nodes and add/delete edges, we can observe an emerging pattern:

1. Get or create cursor

2. Execute a query

3. connection.commit()

4. cursor.close()

Only one of these steps will be different across these methods. After a few of them, there is an unhealthy amount of cut-n-paste code—a practice best avoided when possible. As the cursor business is all the same, we could do it in a single generic function and call a specific function to run the appropriate query:

```
def generalize(func):
    def generic(foo):
        cursor = connection.cursor()
        func(cursor, foo) # <- calling the wrapped function!
        cursor.close()
```

```
        return generic

def add_node(cursor, node):
    cursor.execute('insert into my_nodes (node) value(?)', (node,))

def delete_node(cursor, node):
    cursor.execute('delete from my_nodes where node=?'), (node,))

add_node = generalize(add_node)
add_node('newnode')
```

This replaces add_node() with a new function that does more and does not require a cursor argument. Now every time we call add_node('asdf'), the housekeeping happens automatically, even if was not part of the original add_node() function.

We can do this because in Python, functions are objects, just like any other data. We can create, assign, and call function objects. Here, generalize() creates and returns a *new* function, generic(), that calls func—which we pass as a parameter to general ize(). In a sense, generalize() "wraps" func in another function, adding functionality independently of the original.

Decorator notation

The technique of "wrapping" functions is commonly known as the Decorator Pattern. Python has special syntax for this:

```
def add_node(cursor, node):
    cursor.execute('insert into my_nodes (node) value(?)', (foo,))
add_node = generalize(add_node)

# is same as:

@generalize
def add_node(cursor, node):
    cursor.execute('insert into my_nodes (node) value(?)', (foo,))
```

We are almost done! The last things we must look at are arguments. We have defined generic() to take a single argument, foo. But what about modifying edges? Don't they require at least one more argument? Would we have to write a new decorator, or are we ready to give up and resort to cut-n-pasting? Well, Python has something for that as well: generic argument notation.

> To those who are thinking at this point that "this is more than I cared to know," we remind you that the goal is to illustrate how things are done in the real world! We crafted this example as close to the production quality as we could without losing educational value. We realize not all of this is absolutely essential to this example, but in modern languages like Python, a little initial learning curve goes a long way.

The finished decorator and the resulting class methods are as follows:

```python
def cursored(func):
    def wrapper(sqlgraph, *args, **kwargs):
        supplied_cursor = kwargs.get('cursor', None)
        cursor = supplied_cursor or sqlgraph.conn.cursor()
        kwargs['cursor'] = cursor
        result = func(sqlgraph, *args, **kwargs)
        if not supplied_cursor:
            cursor.connection.commit()
            cursor.close()
        return result
    return wrapper
...
    @cursored
    def add_node(self, node, attr_dict=None, cursor=None):
        attributes = simplejson.dumps(attr_dict)
        cursor.execute('''insert or replace into "%s_nodes" (node, attributes)
            values(?,?)''' % self.name, (node, attributes))

    @cursored
    def add_edge(self, fromnode, tonode, attr_dict=None, cursor=None):
        attributes = simplejson.dumps(attr_dict)
        cursor.execute('''insert or replace into "%s_edges" (efrom, eto, attributes)
            values(?,?,?)''' % self.name, (fromnode, tonode, attributes))

    @cursored
    def remove_node(self, node, cursor=None):
        cursor.execute('delete from "%s_nodes" where node=?' % self.name, (node,))

    @cursored
    def remove_edge(self, fromnode, tonode, cursor=None):
        cursor.execute('delete from "%s_edges" where efrom=? and eto=?' % self.name,
                    (fromnode, tonode))
```

The Adaptor

Now that we have a basic graph that is stored in the database, it is time to think about the connection to NetworkX. This is where the work we did above comes into play.

Conceptually, storing a graph in the database is rather simple: loop through the nodes, store each one, repeat for edges. The actual code is not much different:

```python
def from_nx(self, G):
    self.name = _encode(G.name)
    _prepare_tables(self.conn, self.name)
    c = self.conn.cursor()
    for node, attr_dict in G.node.items():
        self.add_node(node, attr_dict, cursor=c)
    for efrom, eto, attr_dict in G.edges(data=True):
        self.add_edge(efrom, eto, attr_dict, cursor=c)
    self.conn.commit()
    c.close()
```

And the same for the reverse conversion:

```
def to_nx(self):
    G = networkx.Graph()
    c = self.conn.cursor()
    for row in c.execute('select * from "%s_nodes"' % self.name):
        G.add_node(row[0], attr_dict=simplejson.loads(row[1]))
    for row in c.execute('select * from "%s_edges"' % self.name):
        G.add_edge(row[0], row[1], attr_dict=simplejson.loads(row[2]))
    self.conn.commit()
    c.close()
    G.name = _decode(self.name)
    return G
```

Notice the use of the name and the serialization of the attribute dictionaries.

 To get a feel for JSON serialization we encourage the reader to try and compare the output of simplejson.dumps() d to that of str() on a dictionary object. They look quite similar, minus the specific JSON syntax differences. The major difference, however, is that reverse conversion from a canonical string representation requires the use of an eval()—another dangerous practice.

Lastly, it is good practice to provide convenience methods at the module level:

```
def write_sqlite(G, sqlfile):
    ''' Graphs with same names will overwrite each other'''
    sq = SqlGraph(sqlfile, G.name)
    sq.from_nx(G)
    return sq

def read_sqlite(sqlfile, name):
    sq = SqlGraph(sqlfile, name)
    return sq.to_nx()

>>> from sqlgraph import SqlGraph
>>> import networkx
>>> g.node
{0: {}, 1: {}, 2: {}, 3: {}, 4: {}, 5: {}, 6: {}, 7: {}, 8: {}, 9: {}}
>>> sg = sqlgraph.write_sqlite(g, '/tmp/mydbfile')  # storing a graph
>>> sg.add_node('foo')                              # creating a new node
>>> new_g = sg.to_nx()                              # reading the graph back
>>> new_g.node
{0: {}, 1: {}, 2: {}, 3: {}, 4: {}, 5: {}, 6: {}, 7: {}, 8: {}, 9: {}, u'foo': {}}
```

Please refer to *https://github.com/maksim2042/SNABook/tree/master/chapter7* for the complete source listing.

Working with 2-Mode Data

Bimodal data (e.g., election finance data like we used in "Does Campaign Finance Influence Elections?" on page 93) can be stored in the same way as the unimodal data, but presents a special opportunity. As we mentioned in "2-Mode Networks in Practice" on page 100, computation of projected networks is very computationally expensive ($O(n^*m^*n)$), and one of its bottlenecks is the speed of a lookup of a node or an edge in the table. Of course, a well-indexed and normalized SQL database is very good at fast look-up, so we are going to whip up some special SQL kung-fu to compute projected networks inside the database.

Let us assume that the database schema remains the same, but now the `from_node` and the `to_node` in the `edges` table are of different types (e.g., candidates and PACs). We can then compute projected networks with a single SQL SELECT statement:

```
select
     foo.from_node as fromID , bar.from_node as toID, count(*) as weight
from
    (select * from edges where ......) as foo,
    (select * from edges where ......) as bar
where
    foo.to_node = bar.to_node and
    foo.from_node<>bar.from_node
group by foo.from_node, bar.from_node
```

Lines 4 and 5 of the `select` statement are exactly the same—they specify a subset of edges from which we should build the projected network. As the speed of computational scales quadratically with the number of nodes, we should take care to prefilter the network as much as humanly possible before computing the projected network. We run the same filter twice (your database engine will cache the results so it is about as fast as running it once), and give the result-sets different names (here, *foo* and *bar*, for the lack of anything more meaningful).

In line 7, we perform the join on the "inner dimension" of the computation, and in line 8, we exclude self-ties from being counted. Finally, in line 9, we group the results to enable them to be counted in line 2.

The output of this query is a valued edge-list in the form `fromID, toID, weight` that represents the projected network. It can be read directly into a NetworkX object with about 4 lines of Python code:

```
g=net.Graph()
c=cursor.execute(sql)
for row in c:
    g.add_edge(row[0],row[1],weight=row[2])
```

Since the operation to create projected networks is time-consuming, we suggest that the result of the query be cached in a temporary table and periodically updated, rather than computed in real time.

Indexing is very important for this operation; up-to-date indexes should exist on the edges table, both on the `from_node` and `to_node` columns. An index will not fundamentally decrease the number of operations to compute a projected network, but can reduce the time that one operation takes, by an order of magnitude.

Exercises for the Reader

As we mentioned before, this example is rather basic. Here are some improvements it could use on its way to becoming production material:

- Listing stored graphs: currently the only way to inspect the contents of a particular SQLite file is to list the table names. This is not very useful, as the names are a jumbled mess, but is easily solved with a simple function to extract and decode graph names from the tables.
- Indexing: with anything beyond Small Data, indexing would be important for performance reasons.
- Subgraph extraction: so far we provided functionality to modify the stored graph in the database. This is very useful—and we can make this more useful, especially for larger-than-memory graphs, by passing a filter function to `to_nx()` to limit what gets pulled back—a subgraph.
- Traversals: another thing we can perform directly in the database.

Social Networks and Big Data

Big Data and *cloud computing* are the new favorite buzzwords on the block. What are they and, more importantly, should this concern us or should we let them enjoy the fad until it passes?

Our capacities for data transmission, processing, and storage have become virtually boundless and quite cheap. Social networks, as they exist today, are important to us in one primary aspect: as colossal data collectors of human behavior patterns, eagerly powered by the examined themselves, operating on a global scale with near-instant response time. The end result is vast volumes of data, coming at us in a steady stream. We could ask ourselves how much of this data is really interesting, but the answer depends on the particular study. Ideally, however, since we can look at everything, we might as well.

Going back to Twitter as an example, we can scan the 1% sample stream for general trends and topics—anything important enough to generate at least a hundred messages will probably show up. Or, since we are interested in networks, the very active people will make a blip on our radar and we can even see some connections. If that is all we want, storing even a few hundred gigs worth of traffic (in this example, equivalent to a few months time) is no big deal. But what if we wanted to explore trends among the lesser active participants over a few years? The answers would lie in some pretty big data, and to get them, we would have to store and process it somehow.

Now that we have some idea of the scope of the problem, what do we do with a terabyte of social chatter a day?

There are many ways to deal with Big Data, and each process is likely to be unique. Instead of covering a particular process in detail, below we mention some of the tools you are likely to encounter and provide glimpses into the process.

NoSQL

NoSQL is a class of databases that is a departure (sometimes radical), from the classic RDBMS. NoSQL databases typically do not support a query language and lack a fixed schema. They exist in different variations: document stores, key-value stores, object stores, graph databases, and so on. Each variation is designed differently, with a particular context in mind. They are important to us for three common reasons: *structure*, *size*, and *computation*—the same reasons why relational databases are often ill-suited for our purposes. Here are some NoSQL examples:

BigTable
> Google's implementation of a document store, designed to scale across assorted inexpensive hardware. They use it to store the whole Internet. The whole Internet.

HBase
> Open source clone of BigTable, by the Apache Software Foundation. A work in progress, but moving quickly.

Hadoop
> Not a database itself, but the underlying framework for distributed storage and processing, by ASF. The Hadoop project is very impressive and is one of the established standards for Big Data and cloud computing.

MongoDB
> A prominent scalable high-performance document store, with support for indexes, queries and more. Uses JSON documents with dynamic schemas.

CouchDB
> Another distributed document-oriented database, by ASF. Simple to install and operate, and supports MapReduce style indexing (more on MapReduce below).

Neo4j
> A high-performance graph database written in Java.

Hive
> A SQL-like database that can operate on plan text files in a variety of formats.

Structural Realities

The world is an inconsistent and changing place.

It is often the case with Big Data that structural coherence is not guaranteed, chiefly because the data comes from a multitude of diverse sources. Social networks are certainly no exception. Even more so, as the industry changes, the structure of the data evolves very rapidly. Social networking sites continuously add new features and revise data standards. Not only do we have to deal with differences between providers, even the data from the same provider will be changing in time.

Any attempt to coerce, for example, a Twitter stream to a relational schema is futile, because of this structure flux. A single schema for multiple providers is out of the question because of their inherent differences.[3]

Example 7-1. Twitter stream example

```
{
  "in_reply_to_status_id_str":null,
  "id_str":"106394078442291201",
  "truncated":false,
  "text":"Watch this short video from @avaaz for a new path to #MiddleEast peace. #palestine
http://t.co/cPZ8XQU",
  "possibly_sensitive":false,
  "in_reply_to_screen_name":null,
  "created_at":"Wed Aug 24 15:54:59 +0000 2011",
  "in_reply_to_user_id_str":null,
  "entities":{
    "user_mentions":[
      {
        "id_str":"2553151",
        "indices":[28,34],
        "screen_name":"Avaaz",
        "name":"Avaaz.org",
        "id":2553151
      }
    ],
    "hashtags":[
      {"text":"MiddleEast", "indices":[53,64]},
      {"text":"palestine","indices":[72,82]}
    ],
    "urls":[
      {
        "indices":[83,102],
        "url":"http://t.co/cPZ8XQU",
        "display_url":"avaaz.org/en/middle_east\u2026",
        "expanded_url":"http://www.avaaz.org/en/middle_east_peace_now/?twi"
      }
    ]
  },
```

---

3. There have been recent attempts to standardize social network activity streams, though not RDBMS-related; see *http://activitystrea.ms/*.

```
  "contributors":null,
  "retweeted":false,
  "place":null,
  "retweet_count":0,
  "source":"\u003Ca href=\"http://twitter.com/tweetbutton\"rel=\"nofollow\"\u003ETweet
Button\u003C/a\u003E",
  "geo":null,
  "user":{
    "id_str":"179535342",
    "is_translator":false,
    "verified":false,
    "profile_text_color":"333333",
    "listed_count":16,
    "notifications":null,
    "created_at":"Tue Aug 17 14:45:43 +0000 2010",
    "profile_sidebar_fill_color":"8c8c8c",
    "statuses_count":1115,
    "profile_background_tile":false,
    "profile_background_image_url_https":"https://si0.twimg.com/profile_background_images/
307219676/20110423-hebertville-57.jpg",
    "favourites_count":9,
    "profile_image_url":"http://a1.twimg.com/profile_images/1105727684/
Screen_shot_2010-08-18_at_10.40.30_AM_normal.jpg",
    "lang":"en",
    "description":"New Media Artist, Photographer & Musician. ",
    "contributors_enabled":false,
    "profile_link_color":"33cc00",
    "url":"http://mlehmann.ca",
    "screen_name":"meriol_lehmann",
    "default_profile_image":false,
    "profile_sidebar_border_color":"000000",
    "followers_count":231,
    "profile_image_url_https":"https://si0.twimg.com/profile_images/1105727684/
Screen_shot_2010-08-18_at_10.40.30_AM_normal.jpg",
    "following":null,
    "time_zone":"Eastern Time (US & Canada)",
    "profile_use_background_image":true,
    "protected":false,
    "location":"Quebec",
    "default_profile":false,
    "follow_request_sent":null,
    "profile_background_color":"2f3233",
    "name":"Meriol Lehmann",
    "profile_background_image_url":"http://a0.twimg.com/profile_background_images/
307219676/20110423-hebertville-57.jpg",
    "id":179535342,
    "show_all_inline_media":true,
    "geo_enabled":false,
    "utc_offset":-18000,
    "friends_count":428
  },
  "in_reply_to_user_id":null,
  "in_reply_to_status_id":null,
```

```
"id":106394078442291201,
"coordinates":null,
"favorited":false
}
```

 The typical formats supported by social network APIs are XML and JSON, with the latter quickly becoming the preferred choice.

Rather than attempt to coerce data, NoSQL databases embrace diversity. They are very liberal about data structure—sometimes even agnostic of it. We could store the object in the object store and later retrieve its elements; or as a node in a graph database, as a set of key-value pairs, or even as a collection of plain-text files on disk! Many NoSQL databases are designed to operate on structured text files, such as newline-delimited JSON, CSV or XML. Support for new formats is often easy to add.

Plain text is king

The plain-text aspect is of great practical value to us. Suppose we were collecting Twitter data in the format shown above, from an HTTP stream. With a SQL database, a data ingestion flow may look like this:

1. First, learn the data structure and possibly design a fitting schema.
2. Read the stream. For every record:
    a. Parse the record.
    b. Map record fields to an INSERT query.
    c. Execute query, handle unique constraint violations.
    d. Optionally update other tables.

With a text-file-based NoSQL database, the flow becomes this:

1. Read stream.
2. Write record to file.

The freedom to store

Before we can store data in a relational database, we must have a plan in advance. NoSQL's fundamental difference is that we can store now and decide how to interpret or process later—the schema can be anything we want. On top of that, we will not be bound by that decision.

Another important point to consider is this: what happens to the example above when the provider decides to add a new field? Or what if we decide we haven't been storing data correctly? Perhaps, a field we once considered redundant is actually valuable.

With a SQL database, this would be an awkward moment. We may have a live stream consumer that processes tens or hundreds of records a second, none of which we intend to lose. Altering schemas requires a coordinated change in code that interacts with the database, calling for some unpleasant logistics. Now, if we wanted to grab some additional data from the past, the only way to do that would be to reprocess it from a backup —one more dimension of complexity (though a split collector/loader with buffered backup would solve the problem of temporary database loader outage).

A file-based NoSQL solution introduces some zen into the process: the data we collected and stored *is* the backup. We can reprocess it in any way we like at a later time —it's all there, always. In fact, reading and "reprocessing" become one and the same.

Computational Complexities

Distributed computing is a technique of breaking a big task into smaller subtasks, distributing them across multiple machines, and combining the results. One can have a hardware array in-house or turn to *the cloud* and rent virtual machines en masse, on demand, for pennies per hour (each).

Horizontal scaling means NoSQL databases are perfectly suited for the cloud—we can deal with the complexity of the problem simply by throwing more hardware at it. Distributed NoSQL databases are great for Big Data.

Big Data is Big

Some NoSQL databases are designed to scale horizontally to a very large size (petabytes). Similarly, we can keep adding storage nodes.

Big Data at Work

So far we described the various characteristics of a Big Data capable database system, but how does it actually get results out? What is this distributed power good for?

As we mentioned, distributed NoSQL databases are fundamentally different in the way they store and process information. The two important limitations of the traditional RDBMS are structural integrity and capacity. NoSQL data storage and dynamic schemas address the structural limitations, now it is time to explain why it is important to distribute.

What Are We Distributing?

 The earlier days of computing have seen the rise of *parallel processing* (the name Cray, Inc., should have a familiar ring to most). A parallel machine has multiple processors, measured by the tens and more, joined by a high-bandwidth data network (consequently, these machines were the precursors to the modern multicore CPUs). Typically all processors have access to the same data in memory and on disk. One would write their program in a very specific way, with pieces of code that could run as multiple copies on several processors at once and communicate with messages, with each process working on a portion of the task. With the algorithm *parallelized*, the computations ran much faster, reducing tasks that would take days to hours, and so on. The tradeoff, of course, was that these machines were highly specialized, complex, and *extremely* expensive.

In the late 90s, a new idea hit the young web: all the PCs in the world spend at least some time doing nothing—let's borrow their unused CPU cycles and do some useful work, like a small piece of a large problem. Thus emerged public *distributed* computing, with the more popular projects including SETI and the Mersenne Prime search. Each participating machine periodically polled the server, received some numbers to crunch, and later uploaded the result. The server combined the results and queued up more work slices for the participants.

For our purposes, modern distributed computing is a mix of the two approaches. This is how a distributed NoSQL database does its magic on large datasets and why there is a learning curve when coming from SQL-based solutions. The system consists of computational nodes (separate machines or processes on the same machine) where each node receives only a slice of the source data to operate on. The results are then recombined and the process may repeat. With enough processing nodes, any big dataset can be iterated over in reasonable time.

The important point to take away here is that our solution (should we choose a canonical distributed system) must take this architecture into account. No single node gets to see the entire dataset—that would not be practical. The processing code must be able to operate on a slice without knowledge of the rest of the data.

Hadoop, S3, and MapReduce

A distributed cluster of computational nodes needs some way to access the source data. *Hadoop* by ASF makes that easy with HDFS (Hadoop file system) and features like data streaming, for chaining processes. Hadoop automatically distributes chunks of source data between nodes, controls their operation, and monitors their progress via a supplied Web interface.

Amazon S3 (Simple Storage Service) is an online storage service by Amazon. It is distributed and scalable, though the implementation is kept under wraps and to the user it appears as a gigantic disk in some contexts and as a key-value store in others (the key is the filename and the value is the file content). S3 objects can be accessed over HTTP, making it a great Web storage medium. More interestingly, S3 can be accessed as a Hadoop file system.

MapReduce is a computational framework invented by Google and supported by Hadoop. A MapReduce *job* consists, not surprisingly, of a *map* step and a *reduce* step—both names of common functions in functional programming, though not exactly the same. Map step takes the source input, one record at a time, and outputs some meaningful data about it. Multiple copies of the map step work each on a different subset of the source data. Reduce step takes the output of several (or all) map steps and combines them.

This is best illustrated by an example: suppose we are interested in word frequencies in a large volume of text. The map step would receive the text, one line at a time, and output the following pair, for each word it sees: <word>, 1. The reduce step would receive that output, grouped by the first element, and add the numbers (or *reduce* using the *sum* function). The output of the reduce step is the actual word count in our entire corpus:

```
def map(line):
    for word in line.split():
        yield word, 1

def reduce(word, occurrences):
    yield word, sum(occurrences)
```

Something like this could crunch a petabyte of data on a farm of inexpensive servers in mere hours.

Hive

Hive is another project by ASF. It is unique for its effort to bring SQL back into a NoSQL world. Hive operates by transforming SQL queries into MapReduce jobs and presenting their results back in SQL form.

Hive has the important ability to read and write flat files as SQL tables, using what they call a SerDe (serializer/deserializer) to map file contents to columns. There are SerDes provided for CSV, JSON, and regexp formats, and more can be added. The best part is that it can read a collection of files on S3.

Recalling our Twitter JSON example above, this is how we might read a bunch of them in Hive.

Example 7-2. Example Hive input table declaration

```
ADD JAR s3://elasticmapreduce/samples/hive-ads/libs/jsonserde.jar;
ADD JAR s3://elasticmapreduce/samples/hive/jars/hive_contrib.jar;

drop table twitter_stream;
create external table twitter_stream (
contributors string,
coordinates string,
created_at string,
entities_hashtags string,
entities_urls string,
entities_user_mentions string,
favorited string,
geo string,
id string
)
row format serde 'com.amazon.elasticmapreduce.JsonSerde' with serdeproperties (
'paths'='contributors, coordinates, created_at, entities.hashtags, entities.urls,
entities.user_mentions, favorited, geo, id)
location "s3://our-json-data/twitter-stream";
```

In this example, we purposely omit most of the content mappings for brevity. You can see that the `paths` contain JSON paths and the column listing above it maps column names directly to those elements. The location is an S3 "directory" containing our JSON files.

The beauty of this approach is that now our schema is dynamic: we can create as many tables with as many different schemas as we like. Only interested in the subset of the data stored? No problem. Notice how we didn't have to think about it when we wrote that data to S3.

Now we can query, just like any other SQL database:

```
hive> select id from twitter_stream where create_at > '2011-02-03';
```

Because it's a MapReduce job on the inside, it will take a while. Not very gratifying for simple queries, but for large ones it really starts to shine.

But how do we get stuff back? At the time of writing, the supplied JSON SerDe has several limitations—inability to write JSON one of them. This is where an output table becomes useful:

```
create external table tag_network (
 tag1 string,
 tag2 string,
 count string)
row format delimited fields terminated by ' '
stored as textfile
location 's3://our-json-data/output/tag_network/';
```

This will produce space-delimited CSV files in the said directory. But, if we must have our JSON output, we can use a regex SerDe that does support output:

```
drop table hashtags_out;
create external table hashtags_out (
 id string,
 entity string)
row format serde 'org.apache.hadoop.hive.contrib.serde2.RegexSerDe'
with serdeproperties ("input.regex"="\\{\"id\":\"([^ ]*)\",\"entity\":(.*)\\}",
"output.format.string"="{\"id\":\"%1$s\",\"entity\":%2$s}")
stored as textfile
location 's3://our-json-data/output/hashtags';
```

In this example "entity" is actually the `entities.hashtags` element of the original JSON, which is a JSON array itself. This was originally done to overcome another JSON SerDe limitation (inability to handle arrays), but it also makes for a powerful illustration of the dynamic schema principle. Watch this: after inserting into `hashtags_out`, we can read it back in as another table, this time accessing the JSON elements! See the table definition below.

2-Mode Networks in Hive—a recipe

```
create external table hashtags (
 tweet_id string,
 text string,
 indices string
) row format serde 'com.amazon.elasticmapreduce.JsonSerde'
with serdeproperties ('paths'='id, entity.text, entity.indices')
location 's3://our-json-data/output/hashtags/';
```

2-mode networks are just as easy with Hive as any other SQL server. Using this table as an example, this will produce an edge list, weighted by cooccurrence counts, of the hashtag network:

```
hive> select x.text, y.text, count(x.tweet_id)
 from hashtags x full outer join hashtags y on (x.tweet_id=y.tweet_id)
 where x.text != y.text group by x.text, y.text;
```

SQL is Still Our Friend

As great as distributed NoSQL databases are, one things many are not designed for is the ability to quickly answer complex questions—which is exactly what RDBMSs are excellent at. NoSQL is the heavy lifter; it's more about massive computations over full reads than telling you what user RealDalaiLama15 tweeted first thing last Sunday morning and what his friends who only post on weekdays had to say about it.

Whatever the solution, there is often a middle ground between the Big Data backend and the presentation layer for a SQL database, primarily in storing and rapidly querying the Big Data results.

Data Collection

Collecting social network data used to be a tedious, labor-intensive process. In fact, several notable dissertations came out of the researcher's being at the right place and the right time to be able to observe a social conflagration and gather data on it. Social network data collection is, by nature, more invasive and harder to anonymize (since each respondent must provide names of other people); survey instruments had to be approved by Institutional Review Boards (IRBs), and administration of the surveys was tedious manual labor.

In corporate settings, the situation was not much better. While it was possible to gain access to significant amount of data without conducting a survey (e.g., by tapping into an email server log), the data received that way is not a good indicator of trust relations, or formal and informal structures in the organization. Finally, SNA was (and still occasionally is) viewed as a blunt instrument by HR departments (who might mistake a worker with low betweenness centrality for one who is redundant, and lay him off).

Twitter and other social sites make our lives much easier as researchers. First of all, things that are said on Twitter are considered public data. What this means is that an Institutional Review Board does not have to conduct a full review of the study (if you're based at a university), and your firm is not in danger of very bad publicity for the mere act of conducting a study.

If you are at a university or a public institution, an IRB still needs to *take a look* at your research. You must state that you are using *publicly available data* that is not covered under the Human Subjects Research rules, and you should get a dispensation to begin research. In a private company, you are not required to conduct an IRB review (hardly anyone does), but serious ethics violations can have long-ranging fallout; I would urge for an independent ethics review to be conducted as part of due diligence.

Do not use the word *exempt* when talking to an IRB. It means something completely different in IRB legalese.

A Note on the Ethics of Data Collection

Since we have touched on the ethics of data collection, I *must* make a few points to that end:

- Collecting data on human beings *affects their lives*, in hard-to-perceive subtle ways (e.g., collecting tweets), or in direct and powerful ways (e.g., when an HR department makes layoff decisions, or when a drone strike is targeted).

- People are aware that data collection affects their lives. They will manipulate data collection if they think it'll improve their image in one way or another.

- Therefore, you cannot trust people to give you good data. No serious decisions should ever be made on SNA data without it being corroborated from a number of other sources. Actually, this applies to all data, if it is to be used ethically.

The Old-Fashioned Way

In the "bad old days" of Social Network Analysis, when we were still a fringe subfield of sociology, before Twitter and Facebook, before large datasets were practically jumping into the hands of researchers, data was collected by painstakingly administering surveys to small numbers of respondents.

Figure A-1 shows a sample social network questionnaire from a software tool widely used in the late 1990s/early 2000s. Note that the questionnaire is not anonymous—and collection of network data, by definition, cannot be anonymous. After entering their own name (which is liable to produce typos and other errors), the user is asked to click on lots of checkboxes corresponding to the strength of their relationship with other respondents.

This strategy can only work for very small groups—the response rate on any survey drops precipitously with the number of questions asked; you cannot reasonably expect anyone to answer more then 50-100 relationship questions. Even with this painstaking work (recruiting respondents, configuring the survey, administering informed consent forms, etc.,), the data only represents a tiny snapshot of what real interactions look like —and this snapshot is frozen in time, with no hint of dynamics.

The other historically employed strategy is to embed an anthropologist observer in the target population; the observer then recorded interactions that he or she saw while trying not to interfere with the natural flow of the social processes. Of course, the "not interfering" clause is very difficult to implement, especially if the observer is embedded in a society whose culture or ethnicity is different from that of the observer.

Social Network Questionnaire

Thanks for participating. Please note that the data generated in this survey are NOT anonymous and are NOT confidential. The results will be used in the workshop in Washington. **Important note: you must enter your name in Question 0.**

When you're done, press the "Submit" button. Thanks for your help.

Q0. What is **your name**:

Q1. Using the checkboxes below, please indicate **who you have heard of or know about** among the participants of the workshop.

Q2. Check off the names of the **people you know**. By "know" I mean that you can attach a name to a face, you have spoken to each other at least once, and the other person is also likely to put you down.

Q3. Check off the names of people you **have worked with** on a paper or other academic/administrative project.

Q4. Check off the the names of a selected set of people whom you don't know but **would like to know**, based on things you've heard, or their interests, etc.

Name	Q1. Heard of them	Q2. Know them	Q3. Worked with	Q4. Want to know
Allata, Joan	☐	☐	☐	☐
Baer, Justin	☐	☐	☐	☐
Baker, Ted	☐	☐	☐	☐
Bercuwitz, Rick	☐	☐	☐	☐
Branzei, Oana	☐	☐	☐	☐
Brooks, Scott	☐	☐	☐	☐

Figure A-1. Sample social network questionnaire

One of the most troubling uses of this strategy was with the Human Terrain teams deployed by the U.S. military in Iraq and Afghanistan. Originally, the observers were supposed to be embedded in the tribal villages, not wearing a uniform, unarmed, and disavowing any connection to the military presence in the area—and, most importantly, the data they collected was not to be used for any immediate military purpose (e.g., targeting drone strikes).

However, the program quickly found itself in hot water. The American Anthropological Association denounced HTT in October 2007, concerned it could lead to "...compromise of ethics, disgrace to anthropology as an academic discipline, and the endangerment of research subjects." [1]

1. "*U.S. Military, Oblivious of Iraqi Culture, Enlists Anthropologists for Occupation*". Middle East Online. January 19, 2008.

In a report released in December 2009, AAA wrote: "When ethnographic investigation is determined by military missions, not subject to external review, where data collection occurs in the context of war, integrated into the goals of counterinsurgency, and in a potentially coercive environment—all characteristic factors of the [Human Terrain System] concept and its application—it can no longer be considered a legitimate professional exercise of anthropology."

The most troubling facet of the HTS was the fact that data collected by field anthropologists was indeed used as immediate actionable intelligence. While this may have served local operational objectives, it severely compromised the entire program and ultimately worked against the U.S. military's attempts to establish trust and "win hearts and minds."

The authors of this book feel strongly that use of any research tool (SNA or others) without proper consideration for safety of research subjects compromises the field, the methods, and the very nature of science.

From this point on, we shall use all-organic, locally grown, non-violent data sources only.

Mining Server Logs

Corporate email servers hold a treasure trove of social network data. Since every email contains *From:* and *To:* headers, the header information can be treated as a directed graph that can be used for network analysis. Since email traffic can contain various attachments and content, it's a very good idea to conduct content analysis and separate email archives into separate subnetworks. Even simple content analysis can help:

Collaboration networks
> Sending an attached Word document or Excel spreadsheet is a pretty good sign that two people are working together or that one is a subordinate of another.

Setting meetings
> Who sends out meeting invitations and who responds to them? The person setting the meetings is likely to be the boss (or secretary of the boss).

Water cooler talk
> Simple keyword searches for "joke," "funny," and "YouTube" should reveal an undercurrent of a laugh-track in any office. This may be a good approximation of an informal network.

Deeper content analysis could reveal delegation networks, advice networks, troubleshooting networks, and other subnetworks within an organization.

Internally, any corporate entity has the right to conduct analysis of its email logs. However, this data may not be released to the public. Furthermore, the data should be cleansed of any email messages between company employees and people outside of the company.

The best publicly available dataset of this kind is the Enron email archive. It contains data from about 150 users (mostly senior management of Enron), organized into folders. The corpus contains a total of about half a million messages. This data was originally made public and posted to the Web, by the Federal Energy Regulatory Commission during its investigation.[2]

Mining Social Media Sites

Social media sites are an excellent source for SNA data of all sorts and colors. I'm providing just a small list of possible data sources, besides the obvious Twitter and Facebook—there are hundreds more that I have missed. Now that you know what to look for, you will see SNA data everywhere!

Business and Investments

- Crunchbase.com: an excellent source for learning about the startup company community. The database contains (at the time of writing) ~72,000 companies, 95,000 people, and 7,000 investors and investment firms. In the past, my students have used CrunchBase data to analyze coinvestment networks in the BioTech industry (treating the data as a 2-mode network), serial entrepreneurship, and characteristics of highly successful startup companies.

- Yelp.com and FourSquare: both contain tens of thousands of local businesses, and user-submitted reviews of these businesses. Data can be used to find communities of interest in any local area, collective-intelligence recommendations of local businesses, analysis of demand for certain kinds of products and services in an area, etc.

- SEC EDGAR database (*http://www.sec.gov/edgar.shtml*): contains raw Securities and Exchange Commission form filings for all publicly traded companies. Data may be difficult to extract and clean, but contains many nuggets of gold—including board members, investment data, large transactions and contracts, and so on.

Politics, Elections, and Courts

- The Federal Election Commission (FEC) publishes its filings on campaign contributions and electioneering at *http://fec.gov/finance/disclosure/ftp_download.shtml*. As with much of government data, it will require a significant amount of cleaning

---

2. *http://www.cs.cmu.edu/~enron/*

—but can yield very nice results, such as the one we obtained in "Does Campaign Finance Influence Elections?" on page 93.

- OpenSecrets.org takes data from the FEC and does a lot of the data cleaning for you, as well as providing a convenient API for querying data (*http://www.opense crets.org/resources/create/*). The downside to OpenSecrets data is that it is less up-to-date then the data published directly by the FEC, usually lagging by several months.

- OpenCongress.org provides a direct, up-to-date feed to Congressional data. Every vote cast on every bill is available almost instantly (*http://www.opencongress.org/ about/code*). The main API is based on Ruby on Rails, but data is also accessible through a real-time RSS feed.

- USASpending.gov provides data on government contracts and subcontracts through an API and generated CSV files (*http://usaspending.gov/data*). Would you like to know where the taxpayer money goes? What does the collaboration network of the Military-Industrial Complex look like?

Blogosphere and Social Bookmarking

Blogs provide a rich source of social network data—but are difficult to work with due to the fact that blogging is done in a long-form text, with links between bloggers not readily apparent. There are also many blogging platforms (Blogger.com, Wordpress, etc), so uniform APIs for data harvesting may be difficult to come by. Here are some sources:

- LiveJournal.com is the easiest to harvest data from (see "Snowball Sampling" on page 43 for the code). Unfortunately, it's no longer a very popular blogging platform (unless you are in Russia, where it is still #1).

- Technorati.com is a search engine for the blogosphere. Unfortunately, its API was taken offline in 2009 and is no longer available. Site-scraping using Python's URL-Lib and Beautiful Soup libraries is still doable, but is not a long-term solution.

- Digg.com and Reddit.com both provide a "social bookmarking" service—people post links and others vote on them. While the sites are very different in their outlook on life (Digg is more conservative and older, Reddit is a teenager in both audience and views), the APIs are very similar. When many people submit ("digg") the same URL, this can be construed as a beginning of a 2-mode network of similarity. While neither site releases individual votes via the API, Reddit leaked an anonymized file with 24 hours of individual votes in 2010. The projected network derived from the file showed that Reddit is indeed a "hive-mind," where most people vote as a single cluster, upvoting and downvoting the articles in sync.

Twitter Data Collection

Twitter packs a rich data source in the 140 characters. In fact, one can extract no fewer then 5 different network datasets from Twitter. Let's examine a JSON structure returned by Twitter (we omitted parts that are not relevant to this particular analysis):

```
{"in_reply_to_status_id_str":null,
 "id_str":"106066147572584448",
 "text":"RT @BieberTeamNY: RT this if you felt the #earthquake in #NYC bit.ly/x12a34",
 "in_reply_to_screen_name":null,
 "created_at":"Tue Aug 23 18:11:54 +0000 2011",
 "in_reply_to_user_id_str":null,
 "truncated":false,
 "entities":
    {"hashtags":[#earthquake, #NYC],
     "user_mentions":[
        {"id_str":"115485934",
         "indices":[3,16],
         "screen_name":"BieberTeamNY",
         "name":"JB♥NY",
         "id":115485934}],
     "urls":["bit.ly/x12a34"]},
 ...
 "retweeted_status":
    {"in_reply_to_status_id_str":null,
     "id_str":"106065789551001600",
     "in_reply_to_status_id":null,
     "text":"RT this if you felt the earthquake :O",
     "entities":
        {"hashtags":[],
         "user_mentions":[],
         "urls":[]},
     "user":
        {"id_str":"115485934",
         ...
         "screen_name":"BieberTeamNY"},
     "in_reply_to_user_id":null},
 "geo":null,
 "user":
    {"id_str":"185241684",
     ...
     "screen_name":"dancer2198"},
 "in_reply_to_user_id":null,
 "id":106066147572584450,
 }
```

This tweet can be deconstructed as having the following relationships: *@dancer2198* retweeted *@BieberTeamNY* (a *retweet* relationship). His tweet contained the hashtags *#earthquake* and *#NYC* (a *cooccurrence*), and *@dancer2198* also has a relationship with the hashtags (a *use* relationship). A *use* relationship exists between the user and the URL he included in his tweet (*"bit.ly/x12a34"*). Finally, using the Twitter Search API, we can extract a list of the users' friends and followers (a *follower* relationship).

Retweet relationships are very useful for analysis, especially repeated retweets—they represent actual patterns of influence and information diffusion in Twitter networks.

The *use* relationships between people and hashtags or URLs can be interpreted as 2-mode networks, computing a projected network between people (e.g., finding people that are similar in tastes or language but not necessarily directly connected).

The *cooccurrence* relationship between hashtags can be used to build a network of hashtags. If two hashtags occur together more then a few times, one can make an inference that they are semantically related. For example, if #earthquake and #NYC occur in the same tweets 100 times, we may ask whether there indeed was an earthquake in New York (there was one on August 23, 2011).

Finally, since tweets are timestamped and often geocoded, we can learn what trajectories are taken by information as it diffuses through the network. For example, we know that the tweets about the East Coast earthquake were spreading faster then the actual earthquake—giving people far from the epicenter a few seconds of warning.

 There is a public repository of data collected on the day of the earthquake at *http:www.github.com/maksim2042/earthquake*. Have fun with the data!

Facebook

In the face of increasing public pressure, Facebook implemented many privacy controls on its data. As a result, large-scale Facebook datasets became almost completely unavailable. The two kinds of data that can be readily obtained are private ego-network data, and public page data.

Private Ego-Networks

Given Facebook privacy settings, most users can view information on their friends, and their friends' friends. This creates an ego network with a radius of 2 that can tell you something about the user currently logged in. To obtain data on your own Facebook account, go to this URL: *http://apps.facebook.com/netvizz/* and install the app. The app will produce a snapshot of your ego network in the GDF format:

```
nodedef>name VARCHAR,label VARCHAR,sex VARCHAR
34180,Neo,male
304529,Trinity,female
604318,Morpheus,male
701211,Switch,female
edgedef>node1 VARCHAR,node2 VARCHAR
34180,568764524
34180,683355197
34180,1068520044
604318,1826003
```

This file format is not a standard format in the NetworkX arsenal, but a parser can be easily written in a few lines of Python:

```python
def parse_gdf(filename):
    state=''
    file=open(filename,'rb')
    g=net.Graph()
    for line in file:
        if line.startswith("nodedef>"):
            state="nodes"
        elif line.startswith("edgedef>"):
            state="edges"
        elif status is "nodes":
            content=line.split(',')
            g.add_node(content[0],label=content[1],sex=content[2])
        elif status is "edges":
            content=line.split(',')
            g.add_edge(content[0],content[1])
        else:
            continue
    return g
```

You know what to do next!

Facebook Social Graph API

The data returned by Social Graph can be very rich and interacting with the Facebook Graph API can go quite deep. A few open-source projects exist to enable direct Python interaction, including:

- *https://github.com/emre/fb.py*
- *https://github.com/andymckay/python-facebook-graph*
- *https://github.com/gsiegman/python-facebook*

Alternatively, one can interact with the Facebook API using the built-in *urllib* and *simplejson* libraries. However, the details of this are beyond the scope of this book—they are discussed in Mining the Social Web by Matthew Russell and The Facebook Cookbook by Jay Goldman (both by O'Reilly).

Installing Software

This appendix covers the software libraries used in this book, along with installation instructions and examples.

Why (We Love) Python?

The authors share a combined experience in software development dating back to the early 90s. One could say we have seen our fair share of languages and frameworks, both popular and esoteric. It has always seemed that any language or approach you chose gave you a subset of speed, maintainability, and ease of development—but never all of them. From the practical standpoint, educational languages were mostly useless (e.g., Pascal), interpreted languages were slow, "enterprise" languages are arduous to develop and maintain (e.g., Java and its many mind-numbing frameworks). Some of the newer languages were easy to code fast and showed decent performance (e.g., Perl), but the code often grew into a cryptic mess which not many wanted to touch (they also tended to call it a "write-only language").

That said, we see Python as a godsend to all developers. It miraculously combines all the good things we always wanted: it is incredibly fast, makes it easy to develop complex yet robust enterprise-level systems, and is designed to maintain clarity as development expands.

Exploratory Programming

Aside from the beautiful syntax and the fact we now write in 10 lines what used to take three pages of Java, there is one feature we like in particular: what some now call *exploratory programming*. Python is a language best enjoyed interactively and inquisitively.

The default thing for Python to do is to present you with an interactive shell:

```
$ python
Python 2.6.5 (r265:79063, Nov 23 2010, 02:02:03)
[GCC 4.1.2 20080704 (Red Hat 4.1.2-48)] on linux2
Type "help", "copyright", "credits" or "license" for more information.
>>>
```

Questions about the language will arise, regardless of how much experience one possesses. In fact, the abundance of easily accessible information has trained us to not remember everything there is to remember—arguably, for the better. We could look to the great Internet for answers, but we should also remember this: with Python, what is standing between us wondering about a particular feature or a syntax quirk and actually trying it is exactly nothing.

Oh, and it is also a great calculator:

```
>>> (1)
1
>>> [1]
[1]
>>> (1,)
(1,)
>>> type((1))
<type 'int'>
>>> type((1,))
<type 'tuple'>
>>> x = {1:2}
>>> type(x)
<type 'dict'>
>>> 80 * 5 * 20 / 3.2
2500.0
```

That's great, you might say: we can execute expressions and explore the language. But what about exploring code? Python does not enforce types, which means that you may see variables without any indication of what class they really are. This can be unnerving to some, especially those coming from a strongly typed language. The greatest thing about the interactive mode is that you can actually *see* what something is. Very quickly you can learn your way around any code:

```
>>> import csv
>>> dir(csv)
['Dialect', 'DictReader', 'DictWriter', 'Error', 'QUOTE_ALL',
'QUOTE_MINIMAL', 'QUOTE_NONE', 'QUOTE_NONNUMERIC', 'Sniffer',
'StringIO', '_Dialect', '__all__', '__builtins__', '__doc__',
'__file__', '__name__', '__package__', '__version__', 'excel',
'excel_tab', 'field_size_limit', 'get_dialect', 'list_dialects',
're', 'reader', 'reduce', 'register_dialect',
'unregister_dialect', 'writer']
>>> csv.__file__
'/usr/local/lib/python2.6/csv.py'
>>> type(csv.writer)
<type 'builtin_function_or_method'>
```

```
>>> print csv.writer.__doc__
    csv_writer = csv.writer(fileobj [, dialect='excel']
                            [optional keyword args])
    for row in sequence:
        csv_writer.writerow(row)

    [or]

    csv_writer = csv.writer(fileobj [, dialect='excel']
                            [optional keyword args])
    csv_writer.writerows(rows)

The "fileobj" argument can be any object that supports the file API.
```

There are, of course, many other things that can be found about Python objects (and other ways to find them), many of them available in IPython.

A byproduct of Python's interactivity is a type of system design where the deployment and the user interface layers become optional—the system is a library that can be used like a finished system, by programmers and non-programmers alike, immediately. In a team environment, this greatly reduces the amount of development that must happen before a system is useable by everyone.

Python

If your operating system is a modern Unix derivative (Linux, Mac OS X), chances are you already have Python 2.6. If that is not the case, there is help:

http://www.python.org/getit/ http://wiki.python.org/moin/BeginnersGuide/Download

IPython

IPython (*http://ipython.scipy.org/moin/*) is an enhanced Python shell and an architecture for interactive parallel computing. It has everything to make your Python life much easier, from tab completion to inline code inspection and interactive debugging. Just run:

```
easy_install ipython
```

In addition, IPython has a special *pylab* mode for matplotlib.

NetworkX

NetworkX (*http://networkx.lanl.gov/*) is a Python package for the creation, manipulation, and study of the structure, dynamics, and functions of complex networks:

```
easy_install networkx
```

Alternatively, download the package from Python Package Index (*http://pypi.python .org/pypi/networkx*).

matplotlib

matplotlib depends on *numpy* and can be an involved install. There are prepackaged Python distributions with matplotlib already included (such as Enthought Python Distribution or Python (x,y)). Also, most Linux package managers provide matplotlib and numpy prebuilt.

Alternatively, you can download and either install a prebuilt package yourself or compile from source:

http://sourceforge.net/projects/numpy/files/NumPy/   http://sourceforge.net/projects/mat plotlib/files/matplotlib/

matplotlib provides a comprehensive set of instructions online at *http://matplotlib.sour ceforge.net/users/installing.html*.

pylab: matplotlib with IPython

pylab is a MATLAB-like environment: *http://matplotlib.sourceforge.net/users/shell.html #mpl-shell*:

```
$ ipython -pylab
Python 2.6.5 (r265:79063, Apr  1 2010, 05:22:20)
Type "copyright", "credits" or "license" for more information.

IPython 0.10.2 -- An enhanced Interactive Python.
?          -> Introduction and overview of IPython's features.
%quickref -> Quick reference.
help       -> Python's own help system.
object?    -> Details about 'object'. ?object also works, ?? prints more.

  Welcome to pylab, a matplotlib-based Python environment.
  For more information, type 'help(pylab)'.

In [1]: x = randn(10000)

In [2]: hist(x, 100)
```

About the Authors

Maksim Tsvetovat is an interdisciplinary scientist, software engineer, and jazz musician. He received his doctorate from Carnegie Mellon University in the field of Computation, Organizations and Society, concentrating on computational modeling of evolution of social networks, diffusion of information and attitudes, and emergence of collective intelligence. Currently, he teaches social network analysis at George Mason University. He is also a co-founder of DeepMile Networks, a startup company concentrating on mapping influence in social media. Maksim also teaches executive seminars in social network analysis, including "Social Networks for Startups" and "Understanding Social Media for Decisionmakers".

Alex Kouznetsov is a software designer and architect with an extensive technical background ranging from data warehousing to signal processing. He has developed a number of social network analysis tools for the industry, from large-scale data collection to online analysis and presentation tools. Alex received BS degrees in mathematics and computer science from the University of Texas.

Get even more for your money.

Join the O'Reilly Community, and register the O'Reilly books you own. It's free, and you'll get:

- $4.99 ebook upgrade offer
- 40% upgrade offer on O'Reilly print books
- Membership discounts on books and events
- Free lifetime updates to ebooks and videos
- Multiple ebook formats, DRM FREE
- Participation in the O'Reilly community
- Newsletters
- Account management
- 100% Satisfaction Guarantee

Signing up is easy:

1. Go to: oreilly.com/go/register
2. Create an O'Reilly login.
3. Provide your address.
4. Register your books.

Note: English-language books only

To order books online:
oreilly.com/store

For questions about products or an order:
orders@oreilly.com

To sign up to get topic-specific email announcements and/or news about upcoming books, conferences, special offers, and new technologies:
elists@oreilly.com

For technical questions about book content:
booktech@oreilly.com

To submit new book proposals to our editors:
proposals@oreilly.com

O'Reilly books are available in multiple DRM-free ebook formats. For more information:
oreilly.com/ebooks

O'REILLY®

Spreading the knowledge of innovators | oreilly.com

Have it your way.

Made in United States
North Haven, CT
02 February 2022

15550152R00104